# STAGES *of* *the* SOUL

# STAGES *of*
## *the* SOUL

*The Path of the Soulful Life*

### FATHER PAUL KEENAN

CONTEMPORARY BOOKS

**Library of Congress Cataloging-in-Publication Data**

Keenan, Paul.
     Stages of the soul / Paul Keenan.
         p.   cm.
     Includes index.
     ISBN 0-8092-9877-5 (cloth)
         1. Spiritual formation—Catholic Church.   2. Spiritual
life—Catholic Church.   I. Title.
     BX2350.2.K427    2000
     248.2—dc21                        99-57754
                                                       CIP

Interior design by Jeanette Wojtyla

Published by Contemporary Books
A division of NTC/Contemporary Publishing Group, Inc.
4255 West Touhy Avenue, Lincolnwood (Chicago)
Illinois 60712-1975 U.S.A.
Copyright © 2000 by Father Paul Keenan
Printed in the United States of America
International Standard Book Number: 0-8092-9877-5
00  01  02  03  04  05  LB  14  13  12  11  10  9  8  7  6  5  4  3  2  1

# Contents

Acknowledgments                                    VII

**Something More**
*The Essence of a Soulful Life*                      I

**STAGE ONE**
*Lost Souls—the First Step
to Finding the Soul*                                21

**STAGE TWO**
*Falling Through the Cracks*                        55

**STAGE THREE**
*Compassion—the Path to Inner
Guidance and Wisdom*                                81

**STAGE FOUR**
*Tapestry—Discerning a Pattern
in the Pieces of Our Lives*                    . 107

**STAGE FIVE**
*Attic Wisdom—Becoming at Home
With the Eternal*                               133

**STAGE SIX**
*Return—Coming Back to
the World You Left*                             163

**STAGE SEVEN**
*Re-enchantment—Teaching Our
Hearts to Sing Again*                           185

**Preambulations**
*Meandering Through the Soulful Life*           205

*Suggested Reading*                             219

*Index*                                         227

# Acknowledgments

I am profoundly grateful to my literary agent, Denise Marcil, without whose deep interest and support I would not be writing books today. Many thanks to Judith McCarthy, Matthew Carnicelli, Michelle Davidson, Blythe Smith, and all the wonderful people at Contemporary Books who believed in this project from the outset and who zealously worked to bring it to fruition. I am eternally grateful to His Eminence, the late John Cardinal O'Connor, for his unfailing support of my writing and my radio ministry, for his inspiration, and for his personal kindness, which has inspired my life as a priest. Joseph Zwilling, Director of the Office of Communications of the Archdiocese of New York and all of my colleagues there have given me the daily encouragement and camaraderie that have seen me through the ups and downs of authorship. Father Bartholomew Daly, Sharron Charlton, Eileen Fawl, and all of the wonderful people of Our Lady of Peace Church have given me the immeasurable gift of their friendship and support. Susan Zappo has been there every step of the way, bringing love and support whenever needed. There is no adequate way to thank everyone at WOR, WABC, and the Catholic Family Radio Network for the help they have given me as a voice on their stations. If I began to name the names of all my dear and special people—friends, colleagues, board members, listeners, and readers— it would take me another book to mention them all. You know who you are, and how grateful I am for your presence in my life.

Most of all, I am grateful to God for giving me life—not once, but twice—and something wonderful to do with it.

# Something More

*The Essence of a Soulful Life*

There comes a time for all of us when we long for something more. As a boy, I remember sitting in school, daydreaming of past summer vacations taken in the gorgeous northlands of Lakes George and Muskoka in Ontario. As the teacher's voice droned on about some lesson in English or history or math, my mind was lost in the rich blue beauty of the lake where Dad and I had fished. The thrill of catching a huge trout, the clean smell of the northern air breezed across the waters in my mind. Inevitably, my reverie would be discovered, and a reprimand or a question would call me back to the classroom. From my earliest days, I had this restlessness, this wish to be somewhere else, in some creative playland where, far from duty and care, I could just *be*.

I'm sure that's why I fell in love with radio. I can't think of a time when the radio wasn't playing at our house. These days, I suppose, you would say it was a background against the chatter and the work of the day. For me, radio was never a background—it was always the focus, the center of my attention. To this day, if I enter a room and there's a radio playing, my thoughts fly away from the conversation or the tasks at hand and happily land by the radio speaker instead, glued to every word or note. Like my school-day reveries, radio provided me a place to go, far away from daily cares—a creative place of magic and play.

Most of us have, I think, that special place or interest that calls us forth from the everyday into magic. Some heed that call and keep it alive their whole lives. Most of us, at some point, consciously or unconsciously, put it aside. Subtly or not so subtly, we are told to "grow up," to "take responsibility," to "get busy." Now, those are not bad things in and of themselves; we need to learn about discipline and social skills and an ethic of hard work. What happens, though, is that directly or indirectly we are told that we must give up that "childish" place within and "get real." Before long, we are up to our ears in responsibilities, agendas, making a living, coping. The magic has gone. I am amazed how often these days people tell me, "I'm hanging in there," when I ask them how they are. Where is the magic in "hanging in there"?

Sometimes we lose the magic simply because life happens. Cruel and abusive behavior, divorce, sickness, accidents—any and all of these can show us that life can be very hard. I remember seeing on television the faces of ethnic Albanian children, refugees from their homeland due to "ethnic cleansing" by a cruel dictator. It broke my heart to see those starving children, tired, dirty, homeless, and, in some cases, barely alive. The words of Scripture came back to me: "Fear not him who can destroy the body; fear him who can destroy the soul."

The Kosovar children are an extreme and tragic case, of course, but in a way they are not so different from many of us who are fighting an uphill battle to keep some semblance of life within us. More and more as life goes on, we learn to put aside our inner place for the sake of doing what we have to do in order to stay alive.

There is a place within us that longs for something more than the lives and worlds we have created for ourselves. This "something more" does not mean greater accumulation of possessions, titles, honors and awards, or even money. My childhood longing to be back at the lake was not about buying a piece of property. It was about the peace, the beauty, and the freedom that were inherent in my experience that summer and in my later memory of it. There is something in us that longs for a happiness that lies beyond labels and possessions.

What I didn't realize as a kid, when I was dreaming in that second-grade classroom, was that I already had what I thought I wanted. Like most people, I thought that life was all about the world I perceived through the five senses. I thought that I was stuck in that basement classroom with those boring lessons. The only way to be free, I thought, was to get back to that lake. I didn't realize that it wasn't the lake I was longing for—it was the inner aliveness that I had experienced when I was there and when I remembered my time there. It didn't occur to me that I didn't need to have anything else or do anything else or be anywhere else in order to have the joy I wanted.

I didn't realize, back then, that what I wanted—and what I had—was the world of the soul.

Talking about the soul is fashionable these days. Whenever I engage in soul conversation, someone inevitably asks, "Yes, but what *is* the soul, exactly?"

The problem is, the soul does not lend itself to exact definition. Its realm is poetry, myth, suggestion. Genus and species are not its daily bread. Who am I exactly? Yes, I am, biologically speaking, a *Homo sapiens*. In Aristotelian terms, I am a "rational animal." Such definitions do not go to the very heart of me. Recently, an artist friend, unbeknownst to me, painted my portrait. Now *there* I am—me—not a rational animal or a *Homo sapiens*, but me, a living, breathing thing with features and a personality all my own.

That's how the soul is. The definitions we give to it tell us something, but miss the essence of the soul by a country mile. It is like what Augustine discovered in trying to grasp the essence of God. "What does he succeed in saying," the saint pondered, "who attempts to speak of you? But woe to him who does not speak of you at all, when he who speaks the most says nothing."

What is the soul, then? The usual definition is that the soul is the fundamental principle of life. That's what Aristotle called it, five centuries before Christ. But what is life? Aristotle had an answer for that, too. Life is the ability to move oneself. The soul, then, is the underlying source of all motion. This fact alone explains why the soul prefers hints to declarations, for it is the master of new possibilities. Motion—change of any kind—implies denying that things as they are now are the only way that things can be. Recently, a group of middle school kids asked me what I had wanted to be when I was their age. I told them honestly that I had wanted to be a priest and a radio announcer. In my conscious mind, I had no idea how those two objectives might ever fit together. My soul, the master of possibilities, knew how to take what seemed to be incompatible options and weave them together.

The soul, as the fundamental principle of life, is multifaceted. Even while it is orchestrating change, the soul is a haven of safety. Last year, I had the opportunity to watch a colleague go through the various stages of her first pregnancy. I marveled at how peacefully she went through each phase of growth and change, each new stage of the baby's life and consequent intrusion into her own bodily life. One day, toward the end of her pregnancy, I happened to walk into one of the large closets in our office, to find my friend there, sitting in a chair, her eyes closed. "Are you all right?" I asked her.

"Oh yes," she assured me. "I felt I was starting to have contractions, and I wanted to sit quietly and meditate."

That's what the soul does in times of disruption. It holds us quietly even in the midst of our

turmoil and reminds us that this, too, shall pass.
A decade ago, when I was seriously ill, my body
was giving out, but underneath there was a presence urging me to surrender, telling me that
everything was going to be all right.

The soul, for us human beings, is not only
the principle of life; it is also the source of our
unique human life. As human beings, we are not
only able to interact and to feel; we are also able
to experience and to imagine much more than
our senses can offer. We are the fundamental
challenge to the belief that what you see is what
you get. Why, one wonders, do we repeatedly
insist upon limiting ourselves to matter and its
concerns? As I write this, I am looking at one of
the many beautiful stone walls that line New
England roads and driveways. Only a human
being could erect such a structure. Only human
beings can look at a stone, see it for what it is,
link it in their minds with other stones, cement
them together, and create a wall. Only if I am
human can I know what makes the wall I see dif-
fer from the magnificent tree branch that swoops
above it, and know how to leave space for both to
be. That is the work of the soul—the fundamen-

tal ability to take similar things and different things and to know what to do with them. Giving names to things—seeing how things relate as similars and differents and relating them with grace and respect—is the very heart of what we do when we know as human beings are meant to know. Such knowing is the proper work of the soul.

The ability to relate, to compare and contrast things, and to see them in perspective, is the key that opens the door to another dimension of the soul: the ability to appreciate. It is one thing to do something and it is entirely another to appreciate the essence of what we have made. A friend who was experiencing debilitating daily illness in the early stages of her second pregnancy cried out one day in frustration, "I want to be able to *enjoy* being pregnant!"

That is what we all want, really, in our respective circumstances. These days, we spend so much of our lives doing and accomplishing, and so little time appreciating the lives we lead. And yet we want to. We become so busy accomplishing things, running errands, completing projects, that we tend to forget that there is a drive deep within

us that makes us feel that we are of profound
value. Many people go through life hating their
lives, feeling that they are accomplishing nothing
they care about, and believing that love (or prosperity, or luck, or power) is "just around the cor-
ner," but never really here. Interestingly, there
are also people who truly enjoy their jobs, their
homes, their relationships, but who can't help the
nagging feeling that something is missing. They
can't define it or even quite grasp it consciously,
but something is missing, nonetheless; and it feels
like something that money can't buy. That is a
wonderful paradox, because the word "appreciate" means "to put a price on." It is as though
there is another dimension of life, a kind of
country where the things to be gained are not
garnered by overwork, overspending, or over-
achieving. That country is the soul. The soul is
the principle by which we look deeply into
things and discover that things have a value only
insofar as they fulfill a deep underlying purpose.
That purpose has something to do with lifting
up others and ourselves. The soul is the force that
tells us that to touch hearts and make the world
a better place is the only price that is worth pay-
ing for the things we put into our lives.

The soul is the seat of wonder. These days, we often shortchange the idea of wonder. We say, "I wonder," and we mean "I don't understand." I wonder why my shirts aren't whiter. I wonder why I am tired all the time. I wonder why my neighbors act so strangely. That's how we use the word "wonder" today. No wonder we have lost its magic.

The state of wonder is really a state of awe. It is tempting to use the word "reverence" but even that powerful word misses the mark. "Awe" is really the word that most exactly describes what wonder is about.

When we wonder, we are not looking for the answer to something. We are simply amazed at how things are. I watch crows and cardinals and robins swooping and playing beneath their feeder as they dine. I am in wonder at the fun and the beauty and the playfulness of the moment. Wonder is the soul finding the eternal in a moment of time.

I can wonder at something negative or tragic as well. When a dear friend died a painful death from cancer in her mid-thirties, leaving parents, siblings, a husband, three small children—and me—my soul was filled with wonder at how

tragic life could sometimes be, and at how
warmth and poignancy and love could appear in
the midst of such profound sorrow.

Wonder is having at least one foot in eternity.
It is the amazement that, beneath our best of
times and worst of times, there is something
deeply important and significant, something to
be kept and treasured.

We can describe these eternal treasures in
many ways. Like philosophers, we can describe
them as truth, beauty, and goodness. Like the-
ologians, we can call them faith, hope, and love.
As a child in grade school, I memorized a list
called "The Gifts of the Holy Spirit": wisdom,
understanding, counsel, fortitude, knowledge,
piety (or faithfulness), and fear of (meaning "reverence for") the Lord. It was only recently that it
occurred to me that we realize these gifts only
after life has crushed us and broken our hearts.
They are what the soul fixes its gaze upon when
the rest of us (mind and body) is reporting that
all is lost.

Wonder is the door that leads from what we
know by our ordinary means of processing the
world to what the soul knows when, from its

gaze at what is eternally true, it tells us that there is more to life than we imagined.

Soulful living means being fully immersed in the day-to-day matters that make up our lives. It often amazes us to realize that the soul drives us back to our normal affairs. While the soul maintains its focus on things that are eternal, it insists that we bring those eternal verities to bear upon our daily world. In the midst of our often difficult and confusing lives, the soul asks that we maintain a sense of wonder at the mystery that we are and that which is ever unfolding about us. For the soul gives us the sense that there is truly a purpose to our lives, indeed to life itself. This purpose has very little to do with the results that we ordinarily call our purpose in life. I might fondly hope, for example, that my books will be bestsellers and bring in abundant royalties. But if I made that the purpose of my writing, I would be shortchanging myself. For me, "payday" is when I receive letters from readers telling me that something I wrote helped them to change their mind about committing suicide, or got them on the road to saving their marriage, or helped them make sense of what was happening to them dur-

ing a breakdown. To me, that is more important
than writing a bestseller could ever be.

If that's what it means to be soulful, some will
retort, it sounds like settling for less. It sounds
like what you say to yourself when things don't
go the way you hoped.

That's not so, because once you have crossed
the threshold into living a soulful life, your focus
becomes the process of touching hearts and making the world a better place, and nothing else.
There are times when our work draws accolades
and results; there are times when it draws resistance and silence. Every teacher knows exactly
what I mean; sometimes the kids love you and
sometimes they hate you, especially when you
have to correct them or be tough on them. Every
good teacher knows that the best education com-
bines truth and tangible love. If, in teaching or in
any other endeavor, you can honestly say, "I am
doing the best I can to bring truth and love to
this situation," you can continue on, even on the
days when the results do not seem to be there.
Soulfulness allows you to focus on the higher
standard as your goal. On the other hand, great
results and great popularity without truth and

love give the distinct impression that something is missing. Great achievements—money, honors, numbers, grades—accomplished without love always miss the mark.

This is not to say that soulful living means eschewing results altogether. What it means is that the soul asks us not to sell ourselves short in choosing the results we want. There is nothing soulful in the appalling inability of many school-children (and adults as well) to speak, spell, read, and write correctly. Education must choose literacy as one of its results. At the same time, we all know well-educated and highly literate people who haven't a clue what life is about. Soulful living means making choices as to which results or goals will help us best achieve our purpose in life.

Soulful living is not something that we achieve at the end of a process. It is something that we have, in some respect, from the moment of our conception. The soul is with us from that moment and it is with us always, even after death. Sometimes religion seems to imply that life on earth is merely a testing ground for eternal life. The truth is, the soul is with us all through our lives, and every stage of life is meant to be lived soulfully. Even if we have become completely lost, we are still soulful creatures who are being invited to look beyond the ordinary ways in which people think of life. Soulful living implies an inner guidance by which to make sense of our lives. This book is about learning to listen to the things your soul is trying to tell you, even in those times when your life seems to be falling apart.

At first that might seem an absurd thing to say, for when we feel lost we do not normally have a sense of guidance at all, not even guidance from within. On the contrary, when we are lost, we can begin to see that things that didn't seem important were actually wake-up calls from our soul.

The soul is insistent, even when we don't know it is there. A fifteen-year-old girl, deeply depressed, accompanied her father into a bookstore one day, saw my book *Good News for Bad Days* on one of the shelves, and knew that she had to have it. "*Good News,*" she later told me, "changed my life." Was it chance, or was it the soul within her insisting that she look for life, that drew her to the book that helped her? She says—and I agree with her—that her soul was guiding her to what she needed.

The seven stages of the soul outlined in this book are what I see as the natural path the soul takes in leading us from being lost to being fully re-enchanted with life. Though it works in strange and diverse ways, the soul takes a definite path in each of our lives. Seeing this, I think, frees us from having to "take steps" to put our lives together—rather, it lets us know that the steps and the guidance are already there for us. We already know a great deal more than we give ourselves credit for, and this knowing comes from within us. Since our earliest days, it has been signaling to us, beckoning us to heed its wisdom.

I begin the stages with the lost soul stage, because that is where we generally begin to listen to the inner guidance of the soul.

The second stage—falling through the cracks—might give the impression that things are moving in the wrong direction. We were lost, and now we feel not only lost, but also alone and totally removed from help—scared. The soul asks us to consider that our perceptions about our lives might be appearances rather than actual reality.

Are we really lost, or are the cracks we are falling through leading us to something truly substantive and life-giving? Are we really as alone as we imagine?

The third stage—compassion—marks the beginning of the soul's breakthrough from victimization and solecism. It is the step of understanding that we are not alone in experiencing tragedy and heartache. More positively, it brings the realization that not only is peace what *we* want, peace is what everyone wants, even if they do not call it by name. This understanding can turn our lives around and set us on a more outward-looking course.

The fourth stage—tapestry—is where we begin to see the patterns that are forming in our lives, the ones that have helped us and the ones that have led us to being lost. Having begun to evaluate our lives from within, we can also begin to see new possibilities, new threads, and a new pattern for our lives.

The fifth stage, or attic wisdom, is the stage at which we begin to see what the soul sees when it contemplates eternal concepts, such as truth, beauty, wisdom, love, and God. Just as we go up to our attics to find what is of lasting value, we go into our souls to find the perennial wisdom that waits for our embrace.

The sixth stage—return—marks the fact that the soul refuses to allow us to stay lost in ideals. Rather, it draws us back into everyday life, with many of the same cares and burdens we experienced before. Now, however, we have a new place to turn in facing those sometimes daunting tasks. And we have a new sense of purpose in being here. Having seen the very essence of life, we now want to tell others that they need not be lost souls. That may not always be a welcome message.

The seventh stage—re-enchantment—brings our inner and outer worlds full circle into living connection with one another. We see that there is more to our lives than just service, as noble as that might be. It is possible for our hearts to sing with an awareness of our soulful destiny at every moment, every day of our lives.

As you read these pages, may you be blessed with the awareness that you are not alone, and that you are being guided to a destiny far greater than you ever imagined.

# Lost Souls—the First Step to Finding the Soul

One of the great things about my life is that I never know who might be on the other end when the telephone rings, or what he or she will tell me. Fortunately, I like surprises; and life has arranged things so that my thirst for surprise is never entirely quenched. So when the phone rang one July afternoon, and the voice on the other end said, "My name is Dr. Catherine Helene Toye, and I think I am supposed to talk to

you," I was intrigued. Why would a medical doctor want to talk to me? When we arranged the
appointment, I found out that this was no ordinary medical doctor, indeed no ordinary person.
Her book, *My Children, Listen*, proved to be no
ordinary book.

Dr. Catherine Helene Toye was indeed a medical doctor. A radiologist by specialty, she had a
highly successful practice, having graduated from
the prestigious Duke University School of Medicine. She was especially gifted in her ability to
visually scan x-rays and correctly diagnose even
the most difficult cases. A dynamic and vivacious
young woman, she had a gift for remembering
patients' names and for treating them in a loving,
caring way. She adored her two daughters and
was actively involved in all aspects of their lives.

One morning, her life changed radically. As
she tried to get out of bed to begin another day,
Dr. Toye could not plant her feet on the floor. She
literally could not get up. The room spun around
her at a dizzying pace, and there was a shrill ring-
ing in her ears. In an instant, she knew that she
was having an attack of Ménière's disease, and it
dawned on her that she would never practice

medicine again. She was told that she would experience repeated attacks of the illness and that in fifteen years' time she would be deaf. As time went on, she realized that all of her visual and organizational skills, which had been her trademark as a physician, were no longer there. "Suddenly, I had no future, barely even a present," she told me. "I no longer knew who I was or what I could do. Some days, I could not even get out of bed, much less take my children to school or accompany them to events and games as I had done before. My life was literally a shambles."

I looked at the well-dressed, attractive woman who sat in my office and wondered at the poise and the courage that I saw in her face and heard in her words. She had endured what was literally a dizzying loss of career and identity, and now had written a book, *My Children, Listen*, about the newfound experience of God that had become hers in the years since her illness, and the mission she had discovered of bringing spiritual healing to the world.

I have been a priest for almost twenty-two years and a New York radio talk show host for seven. As I listened to Dr. Toye's story, I saw that it was a metaphor for many, many lives I have come to know and touch. It was a metaphor for my own at times. My parishioners, my counselees, my radio and television audiences may not have suffered from Ménière's disease. I certainly have not. Nonetheless, many of us have experienced our lives spinning out of control. Many of us have come to that day when, for one reason or other, we are simply not able to face our lives as we have known them. Perhaps we have lost a husband, a wife, a lifelong friend, a beloved pet. Perhaps we have been fired or betrayed by colleagues or coworkers. Perhaps we have walked across the street and been hit by a car. Perhaps, like Dr. Toye, we have awakened to find ourselves unable to get out of bed due to a physical or psychological illness. Whatever the reason, we have found our world spinning. The world, which was once so familiar to us, seems a stranger. We have become lost souls.

When this happens, we become frightened. It seems as if we are strangers to ourselves. We want to hide. We want to run away. We want to sleep. We want to die. We are frightened and have no idea how we are going to carry on. We feel we have no resources for doing so.

As I listened to Dr. Toye tell me about the first days of her illness, I remembered my own experience and that of countless others who have shared their pain with me over the years. When life strikes us a blow and we feel that we are lost souls, it seems that we have taken the last sure step that we will ever take. Yet I have learned that, instead, the recognition that we are lost souls can be the first step to a deeper and more expansive way of life, the soulful life. The things that appear to be tragedies may rather be the doorways to learning that we are called from deep within ourselves to a unique way of touching the hearts of other people and making the world a better place.

What appears to be a tragedy may instead be a wake-up call. Being a lost soul is often the first step to finding your true purpose and a life that is happier and more hopeful than you ever could have dreamed.

"I was doing very well with my life," Veronica told me. "I was successful, making a great deal of money. I was outgoing, funny, and had lots of friends." Looking at the poised young thirty-something woman sitting in my office, I could well understand why. This was a dynamic young woman who appeared to have everything going for her. "Then one day, about six months ago, everything changed. I could feel my heart knotting into a little ball of terror. I found myself dreading going to the office and making decisions. I started to find excuses not to go out with my friends. I hid. I used to be warm and outgoing, and suddenly I found myself bursting into tears if someone asked me how I was. I saw a doctor, but I couldn't even take depression medication: my body couldn't handle any outside stimulation or pressure. This has been going on for six months. My family is driving me crazy. They keep telling me to snap out of it, to get back to normal. Friends keep after me to go out. My boss tells me my performance is slipping. I'm tired all the time. I don't know what to do. I'm lost. I'm simply lost."

As I listened to Veronica, I could relate to what she was saying, because at about the same time in my life, something similar happened to me. I was a successful young teacher who had to leave the classroom to finish seminary studies for ordination. I wanted to be ordained, but I did not want to move on from the first security I had known in a very long time. When I did, my inner world fell apart. I, too, was a lost soul.

Indeed, for a large part of my life, I was a lost soul. At least that is how I felt. I look back on my childhood as a happy time. I loved the radio and spent countless joyful hours listening to every program and station imaginable. When I wasn't listening, I was "broadcasting," my bedroom lamp having been transformed into a microphone by the removal of the lampshade, my phonograph pressed into service as a turntable while I played my 45-RPM records. That, to me, was bliss.

As I grew older, I came to feel like a lost soul, and that feeling continued to haunt me into young adulthood. It wasn't so much that I was bad. It was more that I lacked focus. I really didn't enjoy school. There was a period of time when I enjoyed sports; but I was never athletically inclined, and my interest soon waned. I often had the feeling that I could never do anything right. By the time I got to high school, I was awkward

and diffident, really shy and unsure of myself. I
got through school pretty well, but had very little focus. By the time I reached college, I had the
fairly definite goal of entering a seminary; at least
my life had that focus. But I was very insecure
and reticent, and it was difficult to speak up in
classes and meetings. I remember one painful
parent-student meeting in which my parents kept
telling me to "speak up." This drove me deeper
into frustrated silence. I really didn't know what
to say.

That's how I felt much of the time through
early adulthood—shy and embarrassed. I did well
as a young teacher: there was something definite
for me to teach, and I knew my subjects (philosophy and theology), enjoyed the students, and
had good relationships with my fellow teachers. I
was a Jesuit seminarian at that time, in the teaching period of the training known as "regency."
When the time came to go to "theology" (the
last years of training before ordination), I was
devastated.

It wasn't that I didn't want to be a priest. A
couple of things were happening that, in combination, helped me to feel even more lost than

before. One had to do with the state of the Catholic Church. The Second Vatican Council had brought a wave of fresh air into the Church—a greater sense of community, a fresh approach to theology, the celebration of the Mass facing the people and in the vernacular. But it also bred enormous turmoil, as hallowed structures and attitudes teetered and toppled. Almost everywhere, seminaries became hotbeds of confusion as professors and students alike wrestled with the role of the priest in modern society. Personally, I went into a heavily academic religious community, the Jesuits, after college, only to find them redefining themselves as missionaries and instruments of social transformation, privatizing their universities, and struggling to understand their identity as a priestly society. Of course, they had every right to do that. It was just that in the midst of such changes, I did not experience the kind of solid modeling that young fellows need at that time in their lives. I felt lost.

The other factor in my feeling of being lost was truly personal. As a young man, rather naïve and lacking in confidence, I had found myself as a teacher and now had to give it up to become a

student again. The next several years, including
the years immediately after ordination, were years
in which I felt myself drifting. I did not know
where I was going or, truly, whether I had anything to give. This continued into my years as a
graduate student enrolled in a doctoral program
in philosophy. Try as I might, I felt overwhelmed
and out of my element. I was thirty-six when I
left the doctoral program, two or three years
short of my degree. I was really becoming a lost
soul.

The road to self-awareness often begins with
the experience of being lost. I am reminded of
the story of the Buddha, who was raised in an
idyllic environment, far removed from the rav-
ages that often beset most people. The legend
about him says that he wandered out and met a
sick man, a dead man, and two men fighting.
These were his first experiences of suffering in
life, and he was shaken. No longer could he live
in his naïve, though perfect, world. There was
no way for him to return home.

The Buddha's story is like that of so many
of us. We come into a world; just as we are learning how to live there, the foundations we have

come to rely on are pulled out from under us. "Up vistaed hopes I sped," recounts the poet Francis Thompson, a long-time addict, "and shot, precipitated adown, titanic glooms of chasmed fears."

The Buddha concluded that human life was full of suffering. Lost souls know just what he meant. When suffering touches our lives, it is shocking, and—what is worse—it brings a cortege along with it: suffering upon suffering.

Many people today live their lives as lost souls. Their jobs, their social lives, their leisure do little to stimulate in them any sense of depth or purpose. One would think that, living in a seminary and as a priest, I would have had a strong conscious sense of purpose. Instead, I was coming to believe that each day was worse than the one before, that life always had something harsh in store. I had grown up around that same sense at home and I tried my best to fight it; but there it was, always at the door. Our relationships with others and with God become shattered and painful when we haven't a clue as to what we can lean on or where we can pin our hopes. Not being able to stand on our own two feet, we look everywhere for props. One by one, they seem to fall out from under us. We feel lost.

The Danish existentialist philosopher Søren Aabye Kierkegaard spoke eloquently of this sensation of being lost. "So many live out their lives in quiet lostness," he wrote. "They live, as it were, away from themselves and vanish like shadows. Their immortal souls are blown away, and they are not disquieted by the question of its immortality, because they are already disintegrated before they die."

Kierkegaard's words aptly describe the hell that we live in as lost souls. He speaks of people "living away from themselves." The turn of phrase is reminiscent of a prodigal son, someone who has moved away from home and cannot find the way back. The road is pockmarked with the ravaging effects of bad experiences.

When people live outside of themselves, they lose the sense of being at home. This state of being is often called "alienation." I remember years ago giving a sermon about the experience of being shattered by tragedy. Afterward, a woman came up to me in tears. "That is just how I feel," she told me. "My life is shattered into a thousand pieces."

The experience of being a lost soul means that you feel you have no anchor, no touchstone for your life. Often, this is why people attempt to fill up their empty lives with things. They are seeking a home in something outside themselves. As a kid, I remember visiting the house of a friend who lived a couple of blocks from us. The house was magnificent, huge, and replete with lovely furniture, televisions, and stereos. As I got to know my friend better, I discovered that his parents argued and drank a lot and generally lived a chaotic and unpleasant life. Our house—attractive, though in many ways more modest—felt like a home. You could feel the love there. Dad's work was hard, my school life was hard, but we had a place to come home to. That place, lovingly cared for by my mother, was formed more by the love in our hearts and souls than by the things we owned.

When life seems like one bad occurrence after another, it is only a matter of time before, in Kierkegaard's words, our "immortal souls are blown away." That is an amazing turn of phrase. It means that we have reached a point where we are totally forgetful of having any ultimate greatness, any divine destiny, any sense of being made in the image and likeness of God. If there is any truth to Albert Camus's dictum that "we come into the world laden with the weight of an infinite necessity," the weight of a lost soul is even more burdensome; it is the weight of the realization that any necessity is merely finite. That is a keener disappointment and more shattering.

This sense of being a lost soul is not necessarily about committing sin in the full moral sense of the term. Granted, a life of sin tends to create the effect of being lost; repeated negligence, in turn, can lead to dishonesty, lack of respect for life, injustice, and other serious sins. But what makes the state of being a lost soul all the more appalling is that it can happen to people who are seemingly doing their best from day to day. All they are trying to do is live, and life keeps knocking them down. "Nobody dast blame this man . . . ," says Charley in *Death of a Salesman*. "He's a man way out there on the blue, riding on a smile and a shoeshine. And when they start not smiling back—that is an earthquake. And then you get yourself a couple of spots on your hat, and you're finished."

I've been there. Many of us have. We've been to that place where life puts those spots on your

hat, and you're finished. Who cares, as Kierkegaard says, whether the soul is immortal? When
your spirit is broken, life seems downright endless, not merely immortal. That feels like very bad
news.

But is it?

There's another quote I love from *Death of a
Salesman*. It's from Linda, Willy Loman's wife.
"He's not the finest character that ever lived," she
says of Willy. "But he's a human being, and a terrible thing is happening to him. So attention
must be paid."

Attention must be paid. There must be Lindas
in our lives who see what is happening to us, who
care, who pay attention, and who try to teach us
to pay attention to ourselves. They reach us while
we are still in that first soul step of being lost.
While they may not personally be able to lead us
all the way out of our lostness, they can give us
a sense that we are able to make the journey and
we begin to see some light again.

While I am always grateful when someone
like Veronica tells me that a book I have written
or a sermon I have preached or something I have
said on the radio has helped him or her to find
the thread that enables them to begin their jour-

ney of the soul, I would rather share with you
the story of a man who did this for me. Over a
period of years he became my teacher, my colleague, and my friend. He was a Jesuit priest by
the name of Bob Lakas, a giant of a man I will
never forget.

Father Lakas was bigger than life. He was a
huge man, handsome, with the demeanor and the
gestures of an actor. A Jesuit and a Yalie, he had
an encyclopedic knowledge of literature, theology, art, and music. He was blessed with bound-
less energy and an imagination that crackled and
sizzled, especially when he taught.

There was no sleeping at the switch in Father
Lakas's classroom. You never knew when he was
going to call on you to answer a question—or to
pray. In Jesuit colleges in 1963, it was the custom
to begin classes with a prayer; and we at Rockhurst College in Kansas City usually began classes
with a recited prayer, an Our Father or a Hail
Mary. Father Lakas had a different idea. At the
customary prayer time, he would suddenly call on
one of us to offer a prayer in our own words. It
was a daunting task for eighteen-year-old boys—
Rockhurst was an all-boys school in those days.

For a chronically embarrassed kid like me, it was especially challenging to find public words for prayer. It made prayer an affair of the heart and taught me that God could be approached at any time and with any words that I could find.

I took many classes with Father Lakas in my college career, but those first two semesters of freshman English were special. Essentially, they were freshman composition courses. Again, Lakas had a different idea. Most comp courses were about writing. With Lakas, they were about reading. "You fellows have to read good books," he advised us. "Otherwise you won't have anything to talk about on a date." Behind that ersatz bit of advice, there lay a core of solid wisdom. Lakas knew that we would never learn to write if we did not fill our heads with Melville, Dickens, Salinger, Wouk, Joyce, Sophocles, Shakespeare, and Agee. He could make us memorize grammar (and he did), but he knew that he could only teach us the art of writing if he exposed our young imaginations to the works of talented authors.

Our writing came to life because Father Lakas made literature come to life. He taught us how

to read it symbolically, transforming our literal
young minds into imaginative gazelles. We read
*Moby Dick* and learned the power of Melville's
circle imagery as Lakas emblazoned the black-
board with multicolored circles etched in chalk.
He marched us through *A Portrait of the Artist as
a Young Man*, inducting us into its complex and
stunning imagery until we inhaled Joyce's pecu-
liar sentences as though they were part of the air
we breathed. In Dickens we discovered what
Lakas called "kinesthetic anticipatory movement"
and learned the power of motion in words.
Reading became an adventure, and our writing
improved steadily. I began to discover that I could
think and that I could write.

In all, I knew Father Bob Lakas for eleven
years. He became my teacher, my mentor, my
colleague, my friend. In time, we taught on the
same faculty, broke bread together, vacationed in
Vale together, prayed together. As our friendship
came to absorb those many roles, there was one
constant. From the first day of that freshman
English course, he saw me for the shy and awkward kid I was and refused to allow me to give in
to that. He encouraged me, corrected me, chal-

lenged me, embarrassed me, cajoled me, prayed for me, and rejoiced at every step of my progress in learning, teaching, and growing toward the priesthood.

Lakas never saw me become a priest. Just before I went to theology, he died of a heart attack in the center aisle of St. Francis Xavier Church in Kansas City. It was a Sunday morning, and he was preparing to celebrate his weekly parish Mass for the people he loved. He walked up the aisle to shake someone's hand, turned around, and screamed, "My Father, My Father," as he fell dead in the aisle. His unexpected and dramatic death was a profound blow. Two evenings before, he had stepped out of a car on the grounds of the college, looked up at the starlit summer sky and declared, "God, how beautiful!" Now he was gone, and my soul was by no means the only one that felt the loss.

In my soul, Bob Lakas lives forever. From time to time, I see those bright, knowing eyes and that mirthful smirk and I hear that booming voice tell me, "Keenan, don't be afraid. Keep on growing. Use your talents. Don't lose heart."

I would know that soul anywhere.

✍

The first stage of soulful living brings with it a
number of ideas worth examining.

1. *Lost souls feel very alone, but they are not
   really so alone.*

2. *The state of being lost is but a first step to
   something new and deep and wonderful: the
   realm of mystery, the realm of soul.*

3. *At this stage, it is important to remember
   that we are just beginning to learn the
   language of soul.*

4. *The seven stages of soul, including this first
   stage, are a part of learning the eternal
   truths of the universe.*

5. *A soulful approach to life allows us to take
   our time figuring things out. Not having
   immediate answers is quite all right.*

> 6. *Living a soulful life is not something we*
> *have to wait for. Nor is it something we can*
> *only achieve at the end of a process.*

Let's look at these ideas in a little detail.

## 1. Lost souls feel very alone, but they are not really so alone.

One of the amazing things about being a lost soul is making the discovery that you are not alone. It took me the longest time to realize that there were other people out there who felt the same way I did. I thought I was the only one, that somehow I was uniquely on the receiving side of life's maleficence. Everybody else seemed to have an easier time of it than I did. Nobody else seemed as shy, as awkward, as diffident, as lacking in knowledge.

Especially at this first stage of soulful living, when you realize that you are a lost soul, it is important to tuck in the back of your mind the understanding that you are not the only one. It may not fully register now, but it's a good idea to have in reserve.

## 2. The state of being lost is but a first step to something new and deep and wonderful: the realm of mystery, the realm of soul.

The essence of the first soul stage is twofold. First, you realize that you are lost. Second, you begin to hold out the hope that the state of being lost is only a first step to something new and better: the realm of mystery, the realm of soul. It is highly possible to be sidetracked at this stage by trying to fix or repair the lostness. You may pretend that you can put your life back together again, that if you just work hard enough, pray hard enough, have enough luck, you will be able to get things back on track, the way they were before.

It takes some doing to realize that the way things were before may not be something we should want to recapture. Often, I hear people reminisce about the "good old days" when things were "simpler," "easier," "better." Especially when things are going badly, we long to resume life as it used to be. When we can open ourselves to the possibility that the reason things fell apart for us may be that we were meant to experience something else, we can relax a little and realize that we may need to stop running around frantically and instead simply listen to what is going on. Dr. Toye, Veronica, and I had to realize that something was supposed to change, and that perhaps those changes had to be made inside of us. Perhaps our inner scope, our inner lives, had become too narrow. Perhaps our souls were inviting us to give them some breathing room. If we listened, we might find out exactly what they meant.

**3. At this stage, it is important to remember that we are just beginning to learn the language of soul.**

As lost souls, we feel very uncomfortable, not only with where we are, but with where we are being invited to go. Once on the radio, a man called me, literally in tears over his inability to communicate with his sixteen-year-old daughter. His marriage had broken up, and he had been separated from her for many years; now he felt

she hated him and refused to listen to him. In the
course of our conversation, it became pretty clear
that he was looking for some tip or advice that
would open up the channels of communication.
I'm sure he thought I was crazy when he heard
what I told him to do.

"I'm not going to try to give you a quick fix
for your problem with your daughter," I advised
him. "But I am going to help you to put the
problem where it belongs. The sad breakdown in
communication between you and her is not primarily an external problem. Rather, it's mostly
an internal one. Before you worry about trying to
reach out to her one more time—which is probably going to end in failure—let's have you go to
your soul with the problem."

To be honest, he sounded like he thought I
was a nut. I persisted. I suggested to him that he
take himself to a quiet place where there would
be no distractions. There, he should take two or
three deep breaths until he felt relaxed. Then I
wanted him to close his eyes and to picture himself and his daughter in the same room. However, I wanted him to picture himself as being
her age rather than his present age, a peer rather
than an adult. I wanted him to ask her what was

wrong and listen to what she said. I invited him to talk back and forth with her, each of them speaking from the heart, really listening to each other. In other words, I wanted him and his daughter to have a conversation in their souls, where they could be just two human beings talking without age barriers and role barriers—really talking and listening to each other. The whole problem with their previous conversations was that they were anything but soulful; they were products of a tit–for–tat world where both sides were invested heavily in their own rightness and in the wrongness of the other. The world of soul reduces all of those differences to the common denominator of two people listening and communicating. I wanted him to see that and to experience that world with his daughter before trying to talk to her again in the outside world. He, and perhaps his daughter, needed to open up the barriers that years of useless trying and failing had created—the world that had gotten them lost. They needed to try something new, something that would take them inward.

I don't know yet whether the experiment worked, or whether my caller even tried to make it work. To date, he hasn't called me back to let

me know, though he promised he would. But I
do know of similar situations in which just this
sort of soulful approach has breached such gaps.
My friend, author Wayne Dyer, told me (and
reported in his book *Real Magic*) how this very
kind of soul-based dialogue helped him have the
most fruitful external communication with his
own teenage daughter. There is something about
the soul that when, in Linda Loman's words,
attention is paid to it, it brings almost miraculous
results into our external lives. Why do we insist
on doing things the other way around? Because
at this stage, we literally do not know which end
is up. It is a wonderful time to learn how to listen, to listen to everything that opens itself up to
us. At this stage, we can afford to listen and
absorb. Later, we can evaluate and act.

Just as Linda Loman warned of Willie, "attention must be paid," so Bob Lakas taught me to
pay attention and not to let my soul stay lost. We
need the Lindas and the Lakases, the people who
are determined not to let us slip away. Where we
see our lives as a wasteland, they teach us to
believe that there is a treasure. They teach us to

pay attention. They help us to believe that our souls can be saved.

**4. The seven stages of soul, including this first stage, are a part of learning the eternal truths of the universe.**

Discovering that you are a lost soul is a painful moment in life. Ours is a can-do, take-charge world that both admires and demands knowing what you want and how to get it. There is no time for confusion. Yet as I discovered—and as Veronica will discover—there are a lot of lost souls out there, people who, while keeping up external appearances, find themselves crumbling inside. They are going through a truly heart-breaking time in life. They feel they are going nowhere and have nowhere to go. Everything in life seems empty and futile.

When people discover themselves to be lost souls, they feel that they are drowning. In point of fact, they are just learning how to swim. Contrary to the tenets of our culture of self-help, it is not yet time to take swimming lessons. Rather, it is time to listen, to observe, and to question. Veronica has reached a point where she can no longer ignore the panic signals she was so successful in pushing aside for so long. Now she has begun to listen to them and to observe what those feelings are doing to her. She finds herself calling into question almost every aspect of her life as she has known it.

Veronica may not know what to call it yet, this malady that has overtaken her. She will learn that this is the first soul step: admitting that she is a lost soul and has no idea where she is going. What appears to her right now to be a disaster is rather the first step toward an adventure of discovery and discernment leading to a life infinitely fuller and richer than the one that is crumbling before her eyes.

**5. A soulful approach to life allows us to take our time figuring things out. Not having immediate answers is quite all right.**

At this stage, it is not too early to hold out a thought we will return to later in our examination of the stages of the soul. When we are lost, the only thing we are sure of is that we don't seem to have a direction in which to be moving. This scares the life out of us. Instinctively, we feel that there is something "not okay" about this. What scares us especially is the sense that our lives may never have a direction again. We start asking ourselves questions like, "What if I can never hold down a job again?" "What if nobody will marry me?" "What if I am sick and have no money and end up in the poorhouse?" The problem is, we jump to these questions right away and start panicking because we don't have an immediate answer to them.

When we discover that we are lost souls, we need to know that those panicky questions are natural and normal. We also need to know that a soulful approach allows us time to figure them out; not having immediate answers is okay.

There's a reason for this, and it has a great deal to do with how our souls are structured. As we move through our soul stages, we will see something unusual about our souls. On the one hand, they are very lofty and high-minded. That's no surprise; we expect that of our souls. But at the same time, they are always drawing us back to the concrete world to have an effect on it. There's a twofold pull to our souls, one that is upward and one that is downward. It means that when we're soulful, we really have two places we can call home—one is in the heights and one is on good old Mother Earth. This means that our souls are always a little restless. If they are focused too much on the concrete and particular, they will call us back to essences and universals. If they are focused too much on universals, they will draw us back to concrete involvement. That is why contemplative monks often have concrete daily labor as part of their rule of life. If they spent all day in the chapel meditating, their souls would long for the world of work. If they spent all day working, they would long for the gaze of the eternal.

Part of soulfulness, then, involves at the same time being both somewhat comfortable and somewhat uncomfortable with where we are. When we're feeling like lost souls, we're not where we used to be and so we're uncomfortable; but strangely, we're also uncomfortable when we futilely try to put our old lives back together. We hope that maybe if we could just go back to our favorite restaurant and taste the food and hear the violins again, our marriage would be all better. How often we're disappointed when we try to do it!

So what's to be done? When our souls seem lost, we need to know that it is important that we become comfortable with being betwixt and between. "Nonsense!" we thunder. "That leaves us in no-man's-land!"

Actually, it leaves us in great safety. Part of the learning experience involved in the soul stages is learning to trust our souls. Our souls know when it is time for us to go to the heights and time to come back down to earth. As we become friends with our souls, we learn that they can accurately read their needs and ours better than we can. I once asked Thomas Moore, author of *Care of the Soul*, how he cared for his soul in the midst of a busy speaking and writing schedule. "I make sure I have plenty of time at home," he said. "And especially time in the garden, working directly with the earth." He has learned that his soul demands just that kind of rhythm.

It's something for us to consider, too, when we find ourselves being lost souls. It is a time when we can begin to watch our souls beckon us back and forth between the universal and the concrete, the sublime and the ridiculous. We may feel like perpetual pilgrims, constantly roaming back and forth, without a home.

The thing of it is, we are learning to live in a new home, a home that is neither "here" nor "there," but both. Especially when our lives have crumbled, we may feel that we are looking for Utopia, the perfect place. How interesting it is to learn that in Greek, the word "utopia" has roots than mean both "good place" and "no place." The home we are looking for is the soul itself. Restless though we are, we begin to take comfort in the call to something new, a new ambience, a new adventure.

Lost souls are really on the verge of adventure.

## 6. Living a soulful life is not something we have to wait for. Nor is it something we can only achieve at the end of a process.

This first stage, the stage of being a lost soul, is already soulful life. At this stage, we often don't have a clue what is happening, things are so much at sixes and sevens. Remember, though, your soul is where you are. At this stage, people usually don't have much of a grasp of having a soul, what the soul is, or how to contact it. But it is there, nonetheless, from the moment of conception. It never leaves us, no matter how much we may neglect it or how far away from soulful living we may have strayed. We don't have to do anything to get our soul, it is always within us, doing its work even when we are unaware of it.

It is important to emphasize this, because we are so accustomed these days to focusing on what we don't have and on finding just the right book or program or audiotape that will help us get what we don't have. It is not like that with the soul. The soul is always there; soulful living is now, at whatever stage you are in life. You already have a soul; all that is needed is to listen to it.

STAGE TWO

## *Falling Through the Cracks*

The experience of being a lost soul, though a soulful experience, is a painful and confusing one. When you realize that you are lost, it can put you into anxiety and turmoil that can seem endlessly unalleviated. It is not the end point of the pain, however. After experiencing yourself as lost, you eventually start to perceive yourself in unhappy and unfortunate ways. Over time, it begins to seem to you that you have been singled out by life or by God or by destiny for an unhappy and unpleasant life. You start to look at the lives of your neighbors, other family members, colleagues at work. Somehow, it seems to you that while they have great and successful lives, you don't. Somehow, fate has singled you out to be denied what others bask in.

When I was first beginning to question the meaning of spirituality in my own life, I started to experience this feeling of being excluded from life's beneficence. I would read books and hear stories about saints and ordinary people like myself who had remarkable spiritual experiences. Great healings came their way, miracles, moments of deep prayer. "Why not me?" I would wonder. Why was I not experiencing anything like that? Did God favor these people more than me? Was I excluded from good fortune? Why did I have to suffer in disappointment while others reveled in the sunshine?

When you feel like this, you have gone one step beyond feeling lost. It is more like falling through the cracks of life. It is the feeling that everybody else has a good life, except you.

It was the same feeling I had through a lot of my school days. People always told me that I was bright, but I never managed to experience that for myself. I watched other people excel and prosper, while I always struggled along. I would have given anything to be one of those kids who breezed to brilliance and good grades with little effort or anguish, or so it seemed.

When you feel that you have fallen through the cracks, it feels even worse than being lost. A number of factors are involved, all of which have to do with what we believe about ourselves and about life. Here are some of the things we believe when we find ourselves falling through the cracks.

1. *You have no solid ground on which you can land.*

2. *It seems that something outside of yourself will stop the floating.*

3. *That which would solve the problem of feeling lost seems elusive and difficult to attain.*

4. *The world is an unfriendly place, especially to you.*

5. *You are utterly alone in your plight.*

6. *Try as you might, you are condemned forever to fall through the cracks.*

Let us take a moment to examine what is involved in each of these beliefs.

## 1. You have no solid ground on which you can land.

Experiencing yourself as someone who is falling through the cracks of life, you believe that there is no solid ground beneath you. Being lost, you try a number of things in order to gain your footing, but in the end nothing seems to work. Try as you might, you see yourself going from one thing to another, hoping to find true comfort and solace and peace. The experience is somewhat like weightless walking in space, except that there is no guarantee you will ever come down to solid ground again.

My friend Julie, a successful Madison Avenue career woman, told me about falling through the cracks as a young child and teenager. "It began on Christmas Day when I was five years old. The day began as a normal Christmas morning with the happy opening of presents under the tree. Sometime in the late afternoon, I happened to hear a thud on the stairs as if someone had fallen. I ran to the top of the stairs. There, crumpled at the bottom with a huge bleeding gash in her head, was my mother. I ran to her, threw my arms around her and cried, 'Mommy, Mommy, talk to me.' Though I had never seen a dead person before, I knew in my heart that my mother was not going to answer me or to get up.

"In the confusion that followed," Julie recounted, "it was hard to know anything for sure. The newspaper said that my mother had tripped over our puppy, but none of us knew for sure what had happened, much less why my mother had to die."

That horrible Christmas incident was just the beginning of a bizarre series of events that would leave Julie and her older sister lost and on their own, their lives spinning out of control. In a family given to hiding unpleasant things rather than bringing them into the open, the death of Julie's mother increasingly became a catalyst for the dissolution of her family. As Julie and her sister reached adolescence, their father distanced himself more and more. In the end, he bought a house for his teenage daughters and moved into his own house, leaving them on their own.

"I stopped going to school," Julie told me. "Day after day, I would sit in front of the television and eat junk food. The worst part was that no one seemed to care or even notice. There I was, a teenager. My mother was dead, my father was gone. I had dropped out of school and out of life—and nobody noticed. I was falling through the cracks at an accelerating rate—and nobody cared."

At length, a Catholic nun, who eventually coaxed her back to school, noticed Julie's absence. "If it hadn't been for that nun," Julie mused, "I wonder where I might be today." Certainly not on Madison Avenue.

Julie's story highlights an important aspect of the soul stage of falling through the cracks. When life forces you from your moorings, you become aware of floating free on your own. Julie lost her mother, then eventually her father, then school, then everyone. Nobody seemed to mind or to care.

## 2. It seems that something outside of yourself will stop the floating.

Nature, they say, abhors a vacuum, and having nowhere to turn for security is a hateful and frightening experience. When we feel that our lives are going nowhere, we desperately look for somewhere to land and something to cling to. For some, it is alcohol or drugs that becomes the bedrock of choice. For others, the vacuum is resolved through a nervous bustling about, filling every moment with chatter, noise, activity, appointments, distractions. For Julie, it was her junk food. For the members of the Trench Coat Mafia who killed classmates and a teacher in Littleton, Colorado, in April 1999, it was guns, bombs, and a violence-based website that filled the gap—or tried to.

When we define ourselves—or let others define us—by what we own, what we do, or how many or what type of friends we have, we are essentially trying to fill the void we believe to be so very deeply ours. We become extremely uncomfortable with the nothingness that seems to be at the heart of ourselves. In a materialistic society, nothingness is bad; possessions and results are good. A void seems like an empty, negative thing, something to get rid of. Frantically, we turn to things outside of ourselves to fill the void.

Yet try as we may to fill the void, we continue to free-fall because the emptiness in the pit of our hearts never quite seems to go away.

## 3. That which would solve the problem of feeling lost seems elusive and difficult to attain.

This is a large part of the frustration of falling through the cracks. The reason for the frustration has a great deal to do with how our minds work. It also has something to do with the true nature of the "problem." Let's look at the mind first.

Our minds are created so that whatever they pay attention to expands. The biblical adage, "As you think, so shall you be," says it well. When we focus on problems, we get more problems. When we focus on success, we tend to manifest success.

I often wondered why, across my life, I would have such trouble putting the "as you think" principle into effective practice. It finally occurred to me that many times when I was trying to focus on manifesting success, my efforts were really masking fear of failure. For example, I was trying to manifest prosperity when my mind was worrying about how I was ever going to pay a particular bill. My mind was really focused on being broke, which is why my affirmations of prosperity were getting me nowhere.

I realized, too, that I often did the same thing while praying. I would ask God for health while my mind was focused on pain or illness. We manifest what we focus on—that's the law of the mind.

People who are falling through the cracks often do the same thing. Their focus turns to the fact of being in the cracks, of having no solid place in life to plant their feet. The experience goes on to become a self-fulfilling prophecy. The more you feel that your life is not on solid foot-

ing, the more frightened and panicked you become. The greater the panic, the greater the
awareness of falling through the cracks. The more
you look for a person, a thing, or a circumstance
to make things better, and the more it seems that
the magic bullet isn't there, the more you seem
to be floating. When I was sick in the hospital
after a close brush with death, the doctors told
me I could go home, but only after all of the
jaundice had disappeared from my eyes. Day after
day, I waited, frustrated because I was still yellow
and could not go home. I realize now what the
problem was: I was focusing on the fact that I
didn't have what I wanted. As a result, all I got
was more failure and frustration, and more of the
feeling that my life was hanging in the balance.

## 4. The world is an unfriendly place, especially to you.

Because you are so focused on the solidity your
life doesn't have, it rapidly becomes clear to you
that the world is an unfriendly place. Everything
is a hassle. Nothing comes easily or without a tremendous amount of effort. Much of the time,

you put out the effort, only to find that the results you had hoped for—along with the credit—go to somebody else.

I know that feeling well, because I grew up around it and carried it with me for many years into adulthood. For all of their many wonderful qualities, my parents firmly believed that their lives had no solid footing. Everything was a source of enormous anxiety and worry to them. Early on in his career, my father claimed to have discovered that a colleague had plagiarized some of his ideas and had benefited from doing so. From that time forward, Dad never really forgave him—though he also never confronted him— and for years bemoaned that man's success in contrast to his own struggles. It was a constant belief at our house that the world was something to be suspicious of, that life was a matter of one crisis or disappointment after another, and that you waited for the proverbial other shoe to drop. At the end of a particular visit home from the seminary, I had a conversation with my mother, in the course of which she told me that she didn't feel that she belonged anywhere, that she didn't have any friends, that she didn't want to be both-

ered with the people who wanted to be friends,
and that no one understood her. I felt sad, because both Mom and Dad had much to be proud
of and had every reason to be happy. Within a
few years of that conversation, Mom would be
dead of cancer, and Dad would be left wondering how to live without her, and why they had
been denied the happy retirement they had so
looked forward to.

As the years went by, I thought a great deal
about Mom and Dad and how life always seemed
to them to be unfriendly. Even though I had
caught some of the same bug myself, I often
scratched my head at their approach to life. What
amazed me most of all was the fact that their
often negative attitude coexisted with an unshak-
able religious faith. Mom and Dad were Sunday
churchgoers who never missed, devout Catholics
who made novenas and said the rosary every day
of their married lives. Yet, somehow, their religious beliefs failed to translate into a more affable attitude about the world they lived in and
about the people who lived there with them.
They had their faith and treasured it, but some-

how were always looking over their shoulders for fear that life would once again strike them a blow.

### 5. You are utterly alone in your plight.

That conversation with my mother on the eve of my returning to the seminary revealed that she believed that she belonged nowhere and felt very much alone in life. By no means was she a misanthrope; in fact, she was a socially charming and gracious person who enjoyed entertaining and did it well. But over the years my mother developed a lifestyle that left her increasingly isolated and lacking in companionship. She and Dad doted on each other and were each other's favorite companion. But the increasingly sad fact was that day in and day out my Dad was the only person Mom saw all day long, especially after I left home. Several moves had bred the realization that friends came and went. The growing feeling that life was constantly hurling challenges gave rise to the growing belief that she and Dad were "you and me against the world." People who tried to be friends were "too much bother" or "too nosy." Like all people who find themselves alone with life crumbling under their feet, Mom gradually came to believe that no one could understand or care about her situation.

## 6. Try as you might, you are condemned forever to fall through the cracks.

The horrible fear when you are falling through the cracks is that you will never be able to stop. So much of your life experience has to do with seeing yourself increasingly put upon by life, by others, sometimes, it seems, even by God. It becomes very hard to imagine your life being otherwise, for the weight of the past appears insurmountable. It becomes clear that the future will be just like the past, that you will spend the rest of your life drifting, failing, and being humiliated.

*✑*

These six beliefs amount to a pitiful and self-perpetuating view of ourselves as people who are constantly adrift in life and ever will be. We try something new, all the while hoping against hope that this spouse, this medicine, this program, this book will be the one that will move us away from the chain of trial and error that has become our sad identity.

What would it be like if we were to break out of the cycle of falling through the cracks? What would we believe instead of the six ideas I have just outlined?

**1. Although it feels as if you have no solid ground on which to land, there is a place where you can go—a place called soul.**

No matter how many times you have tried and failed, no matter where you have gone or what you have done, you still have within you a soul, a principle of life. You are not the sum and substance of what you have done, where you have come from, or what others have done to you or said about you. Thanks to your soul, you are free to think differently, to see yourself independently of your history and your labels, whether self-imposed or imposed by others.

As I write these words, I am looking at a newspaper clipping about my friend Sister Ave

Clark. Someone sent it to me in the mail, and it tells yet another heartrending story of the courageous and beautiful love Sister Ave embodies through her Heart to Heart Ministries. Sister Ave is a victim of sexual abuse and suffers daily from depression. Yet as she told me one Saturday morning while we were preparing to give a retreat together, "God takes my little brokenness and uses it to help others." Indeed, this quiet woman spends her days and nights talking with men and woman who suffer from various forms of abuse, helping them through lonely days and sleepless nights to find peace in the pain of their shattered lives. Sister Ave decided long ago that there was more to herself than her brokenness, and she decided to spend her life loving God and helping people like herself to love him as well.

## 2. Nothing outside of you is going to eliminate the pain of falling through the cracks.

All of our efforts at looking for someone or something to fill up the hole we feel inside us fail, because individually and together they cannot fill the infinite longing that lies inside us. Years ago, when I was a freshman in high school, Father Bob Sullivan made us memorize this phrase: "Our search for happiness is a search for God." Try as we might to find satisfaction in the latest fashions, music systems, computers, cars, shows, sexual attractions, and so on, we always end up being disappointed. The French existentialist Jean-Paul Sartre described human beings as always trying to fill up a hole. Instead of being content with our freedom, he said, we are always trying to limit it by having something, doing something, being something. Sartre felt that human life was an absurd tug-of-war between trying to be free on the one hand and trying to be somebody on the other. His philosophy, though drastically incomplete, describes fairly accurately how many of us live. On the one hand, we want our freedom. On the other, we are trying to fill ourselves up with things from outside ourselves.

The essential feature of soulful living is realizing that life is fundamentally an inner game, not an outer game. Once we see ourselves primarily

as soulful beings, we realize that the most important thing about us is our soul, that principle of
life and self-motion that contains the very essence
of who we are. Once it dawns on us that our soul
is there from the moment of conception, our way
of looking at life is changed forever. Our bodies
come and go, they increase, decrease, move, and
age; but our souls are always there, giving them
life, guiding them, directing them, giving them
unity and coherence. Realizing that, we can see
how foolish it is for us to focus our attention first
and foremost on things outside of ourselves, and
only secondarily and occasionally—if at all—
upon our souls. We are conditioned to pile up
this thing, that thing, riches, jobs, honors, and
relationships, all the while forgetting why we
want them. Instead, the secret is to look within,
where we already have everything we need, and
from there allow it all to manifest in the outer
world.

When I had the feeling of falling through
the cracks, it took a great deal of inner work to
sort through what I wanted. For me, it took therapy, meditation, reading, and a lot of prayer and

reflection. On the outside, my opportunity to become a priest of the Archdiocese of New York, to get into radio, and to write books seemed to come along serendipitously. But, in fact, once my soul saw that I was prepared to put it first and to take it seriously, it drew those opportunities in my direction. Inner first, then outer—that's the rule of the soul.

**3. Once we determine to let the soul be our bedrock and to put it first, our lives develop an ease and an effortlessness that wasn't there before.**

Instead of focusing on what we don't have, soulful living puts the focus on the soul itself—the kingdom of God within us. The soul is the realm of possibility and is the center of our power to shape our present and our future. The soul holds our capacities for knowing, loving, and choosing; notwithstanding obstacles and appearances, it keeps us steadfastly advancing toward the goals we imagine. Instead of struggling and straining as though we were on our own, trying everything we can think of, we trust the inner guidance we receive and find ourselves directed to the people, places, and things that are right for us.

## 4. When we live soulfully, the world no longer seems hostile and unfriendly.

Instead of feeling like we are falling through the cracks, we come to lose the sense that we are victims of a whimsical world whose humor often seems to turn against us. Living soulfully, we know that we are putting our primary focus on what cannot be taken away, and that the values that we hold dearest in life, we already hold in abundance. Externals may come and go, tragedies may occur, and we will have bad days along with good days. We will still feel pain and loss, and we will grieve and weep. Knowing that the soul comes first, we will come to absorb our grief and loss into a higher realm, where the very essence of things lies—an essence which cannot be taken away.

It was a warm June night in 1962 when Tom, who had recently graduated from high school, put his car on a jack and went underneath it to do some repairs. In a terrifying second the jack slipped and the car fell, crushing Tom's skull against the pavement. He was left slightly brain damaged, blinded in one eye, and somewhat speech impaired.

What a difference from the popular, handsome young man of high school days. I hadn't known Tom very well—he was a year ahead of me in school, and juniors and seniors were worlds apart. In my freshman year, I had bought some of his used textbooks and had seen him working in the Thriftway from time to time. But somehow, after the accident, he and I became friends. We would go to each other's houses, listen to records, play chess, and talk. It was Tom who introduced me to the music of *West Side Story*.

Tom was very honest about his accident and the limitations it imposed on him. But I never heard him become bitter or lose his will to live. Instead, he was determined to make the most of what life offered him. It must be thirty-five years since I have seen him, but my last memory of him was of his courting a beautiful young woman named Sandra, who appeared to be ready to spend her life with this magnificent young man. When life dealt Tom an evil blow, he went within and found his dearest values and believed in them.

## 5. The feeling of being alone often makes us aware of being unique and having a mission and purpose in the world.

It always seemed a shame to me that my mother wasn't able to see how much life had given her and how much she had brought to the world. I do think that on the day of her death, she was given a glimpse of it. When Dad met me at the airport and took me to her room in the hospital, Mom came out of a coma, looked at Dad and me, called us by name, and said, "Now it is complete." I like to think that at that moment she felt some soulful satisfaction in being a wonderful wife and mother.

When I thought back to that poignant conversation we had had during that visit home, I wondered if my mother's sense of loneliness and futility were not really just a normal part of what many of us feel when we are singularly dedicated. When you find your purpose on earth and dedicate your life to it, it sometimes loses its glamour. Often, you become aware of all the things you might have done instead. Mom always wanted to be a lawyer and regretted not having had the opportunity to do so. When your energies are focused on doing your job well, you can sometimes have very little energy available for people when they reach out in friendship, and yet you wish those relationships could be there. The day-to-day accomplishment of what needs to be done can leave you feeling unimportant and unappreciated.

It is important, though not always easy, to go down beneath all that and to learn to revel in the soul itself. The discouraging voices that we hear are an invitation to find that kingdom deep within, the one that never fades or tarnishes no matter how much our daily life might lose its luster. We must remember that those lackluster days are meant to be reminders of what we are here for. They are not necessarily meant to drive us away from where we are to some imagined paradise. They are meant to lead us to the joy of the paradise within.

## 6. The feeling of falling through the cracks carries with it both truth and illusion.

The truth is that we are being pulled away from moorings which, however much we love them, are not the best places for us to be. The illusion is in the feeling that we are merely drifting. In our confusion, we may feel that we are getting farther away from a purposeful life. In reality, we are being invited to watch every moment for the intimations it brings us, and at the same time we are being asked to put ourselves (through reading, attention, and meditation) in the presence of the values that are most universal and dearest to us. Their names are honesty, truth, love, beauty, goodness, freedom, and service. They are the hallmarks of the soul. As we immerse ourselves in them and watch ourselves being led back to them, we discover the truth about ourselves. We are not free-floating as we thought. We are finding the only solid ground there is.

As much as it seems to be a further condemnation to the state of being lost, this second soul stage—the feeling that you are falling through the cracks of life—can lead you to the first ray of hope you may have had for a very long time. After years of praying about my life and reading tons of self-help literature, I realized that not only did I feel that I was more lost than anyone I knew, but that I was slipping, slipping, slipping. One day, a question found its way into my heart: "Why, after all my praying and reading, do I not have peace?" The question stung me between the eyes. I realized that I did not have peace because until then I had not been aware that it was peace of soul that I was looking for. I thought I was looking for someone, a break, a job, a fortune, an idea. What I was looking for was peace. Now I had a basis for moving ahead. I could stop being a lost soul, and realize that what I was seeking was not something outside, but something inside. I stopped falling through the cracks the day I realized that there was light at the end of the tunnel. I had completed the second stage of the soul.

# Compassion—the Path to Inner Guidance and Wisdom

The moment when you realize that peace is the only true desire of your heart is a defining moment in life. No longer do you feel condemned to float through life. There is something that you want, and it is not a title or a possession or a pot of gold. Rather, it is something within, intimate and deep. What is interesting is that, while you might think that such an experience would further isolate you, it doesn't. Ironically, turning within takes you to the heart, not only of your own experience, but of everyone's. You begin to discover that it is not only you who are searching for peace; so is everyone. That is a startling revelation, and it may even appear to be untrue. We see in our world many people—colleagues, family members, leaders of nations— who seem to want the exact opposite of peace. Indeed, they seem to thrive on conflict. Repeatedly, writers commenting on the political hot spots of the world have remarked at how ceasefires and peace treaties are so tenuous. It almost seems that people are more comfortable in times of war than they are in times of peace. How can I say that everyone wants peace?

The answer is one of ends and means. We do not always know the best means of attaining what we want. Years ago, when some people betrayed me, my first instinct was to get revenge on them. I thought that by getting even with them, I would feel better. I'm glad I didn't give in to those impulses, because they would never have given me the peace I wanted. I did what we often do when we make mistakes in life: I misidentified the right means to the end. I was tempted to

choose means (revenge) that appeared to lead—
but would not truly lead—to the peace I wanted
in my life.

Sometimes we hear people say that our goal
in life is happiness. I disagree, and I think it is
more than a question of semantics. Peace and
happiness are not the same thing. Indeed, a person can be at peace even in the midst of great
unhappiness. I think of my dear friend Mildred,
a beautiful soul who has battled back three times
from deadly cancer. Hers is not a storybook life;
it includes surgeries, chemotherapy, comas, unbe-
lievable pain, and numerous complications. The
amazing part of the story is Mildred's deep and
lasting peace through it all. When she was first
diagnosed with cancer, her doctor broke the news
to her in a very abrupt manner. "The first thing
I did," she said, "was to throw him out of the
room. When he had gone, I put my head on my
pillow and prayed, 'Dear God, thank you for
making me such a strong woman.' I put my head
on my pillow and fell asleep."

That peace has been the hallmark of Mildred's
three successful bouts with cancer. Through it all,
she not only has maintained that inner peace, but

also has spent her time helping others to achieve it as well, through her church and through numerous charitable works. She maintains her own peace and shares it with others. Her life is not about seeking happiness, but it is most certainly about seeking and giving peace.

When you realize that peace is what you are looking for—that it is what all of us are looking for—the realization can turn your life around. This is true even in circumstances of poor health, such as Mildred's, and even when the important relationships in your life have gone awry. Patrick, a young businessman, picked up the phone one morning to call me after reading my book *Good News for Bad Days: Living a Soulful Life*. He had been married ten years when he discovered that his wife was seeing another man. He had read my section on marriage restoration and had determined then and there to try to get hold of me. He persisted; when we talked, he tearfully described his situation. More than anything else, both for himself and for his young son, he wanted to get his marriage back on track. It was not clear whether his wife, whom he had asked to leave the house, shared similar feelings, although they talked every day. As he poured out his anger at his wife for what she had done, it began to dawn on him that this anger, though in many ways legitimate, was not what he really wanted.

"What do you want?" I asked him.

"I want my marriage back," was his immediate reply.

"But why?"

"I want peace in my house, for myself and my son. If she would only come back, we could have peace."

"Let me ask you something, Patrick. Why would your wife want to come back to a house where there is no peace? Perhaps peace is what she is looking for, too. Perhaps that's why she had an affair. Until you're at peace, there is no reason for her to come back. She may choose not to come back, or she might return, who knows? But if you want to save your marriage, you yourself must be at peace, regardless of what happens or what she does or does not do."

I shared with him my belief that as we explored his self, looked at his values, and observed his behavior, we could also pray that God would guide us in the right directions. His work on his marriage, I told him, should not be about changing his wife and certainly not about punishing her. It should be about looking at himself with the help of God.

Patrick caught his breath. It was the first time he had realized that perhaps he and his wife really wanted the same thing—peace. As angry as he was with her and as betrayed as he felt, he began to feel compassion for her. He also began to understand that perhaps the breakup of their marriage was not exclusively her fault. He had no control over what would bring her peace or how she would choose to pursue it. The only control he had was over his own heart and soul, over his own desire for peace. That was where his focus needed to be.

Like many of us, Patrick had to move past blaming someone else for his problems. In addition, it would not be enough for him to focus entirely on blaming himself. Realizing for the first time that perhaps his wife wanted what he wanted—inner peace—Patrick began to understand his wife in a new way. He still felt hurt and betrayed, but he could look at her with compassion and understanding. He also learned that he had to focus on his own inner peace, not on telling her what to do or how to achieve hers. If their reunion were going to happen, it would have to come as the free movement of both of their souls.

There is one other thing Patrick needs to learn. He knows it a little from what has happened, but now he needs to face it head-on. The peace that he is seeking is a deep and abiding peace, not a short-term peace. Until now, Patrick has assumed that peace was the product of compromises, right responses, the cooperation of other people, and even a degree of luck. Now, he needs to understand that none of these things is going to bring him what he wants. In fact, tending to them has brought him what he doesn't want. Like all of us, Patrick needs to think in terms of a peace that transcends good days and bad days, successes and mistakes, the decisions of others, and the smiles of Lady Luck. Now that his heart is touched by compassion, he can see that his wife is a good person even though he believes she has made mistakes and done something that is wrong. The soul stage of compassion allows him to turn this understanding upon himself as well, and to realize that deep and abiding love and peace are not the products of anything but themselves. They must be seen and experienced, not created. Indeed, it is inner peace that guides and governs the outer aspects of life.

When he first learned of his wife's affair, Patrick not only felt lost, he felt his whole life as a person, as a husband, and as a parent was falling apart. Typical of someone falling through the cracks, he kept looking outside of himself to assign blame and to fix his life. As he came to understand what he truly wanted (peace) was not anything that someone else could provide, he began to realize that his wife was searching for exactly the same thing. That helped him to understand better what she was doing and to have compassion for her.

Moving toward compassion led Patrick to a new set of beliefs that we need to consider if we are to deepen in soulfulness.

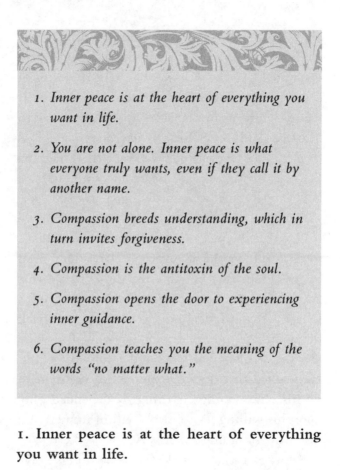

1. *Inner peace is at the heart of everything you want in life.*

2. *You are not alone. Inner peace is what everyone truly wants, even if they call it by another name.*

3. *Compassion breeds understanding, which in turn invites forgiveness.*

4. *Compassion is the antitoxin of the soul.*

5. *Compassion opens the door to experiencing inner guidance.*

6. *Compassion teaches you the meaning of the words "no matter what."*

## 1. Inner peace is at the heart of everything you want in life.

It usually takes a while for us to learn this, just as it takes a while for us to learn that our everyday experience is not the only dimension in which we live. Like Martha in the biblical story, who exhausted herself with worry about the cares of life, we upset ourselves about many things. It seems odd to us in that story to hear Jesus say to Martha, "only one thing is necessary," but it is true. Behind everything we want there lies the desire to have peace of heart and soul, and we believe that what we want will give us that peace.

It takes a good amount of living before we realize that the peace we seek is already available to us in the depths of our souls. We simply need to get in touch with it and stop doing things that keep us from experiencing it. When he began his journey toward healing his marriage, Patrick thought that he would have peace only if his wife saw the error of her ways and returned to him. He learned that his inner peace did not depend on his wife's doing anything. It depended only upon his willingness to look within himself and foster the soulfulness that was already there.

Most of us have made the same mistake. We do it for a couple of reasons. One is that we tend to define peace negatively, as the absence of conflict. The truth is we can have deep and abiding peace in the midst of terrible conflict. The peace prayer of Saint Francis of Assisi asks that we may be instruments of peace specifically in the midst of hatred, doubt, injury, despair, sadness, and darkness. It does not ask that those difficult circumstances be taken away. It asks that we radiate peace when we are confronted with them. Contrary to popular belief, peace does not necessarily (or often) mean that there is no conflict. Peace is that condition of soul by virtue of which we experience and maintain our integrity in the face of profoundly painful and divisive conditions.

The other reason that we are confused about peace is that, like Patrick, we assume that our being at peace depends upon someone else's doing something. Remember, a soul is something you get at the moment of conception. From that moment it is yours and remains so always. Living soulfully does not depend on someone else changing his or her behavior. It depends on your willingness to affirm and to live by your soul's eternal qualities. Once Patrick stopped expecting his wife to change and focused instead on taking responsibility for himself, he was truly able to work on his marriage.

**2. You are not alone. Inner peace is what everyone truly wants, even if they call it by another name.**

It took a little prodding, but eventually it began to dawn on Patrick that his wife had her affair for a reason. She, too, thought that she was going to find peace through someone else, who would fill up her empty soul and make her happy. Previously, she had looked to Patrick for that and he had failed her, or so she thought. She met another man who she found attractive and whose love seemed to fulfil her. Patrick felt betrayed until he understood that both of them had done exactly the same thing. Realizing that, he was able to understand why she left him, since she felt betrayed as well. Once he began to see that, he was freer to stop focusing on his wife and to start focusing on how best to find his own inner peace.

**3. Compassion breeds understanding, which in turn invites forgiveness.**

As Patrick confronted the obstacles within himself to his own experience of inner peace, he slowly began to understand his wife's pain along-

side his own. He still had a good deal of hurt,
anger, rage, and blame in his repertoire; but now
he could begin to grasp that what he was feeling
about his wife was similar to what she was feeling about him. He came to realize that he had
fostered attitudes and taken actions that had
caused her to be hurt and angry, and that if there
were to be any hope for their marriage, he had to
change those attitudes and behaviors.

Interestingly enough, at the same time, Patrick
made beginning efforts at sharing with his wife
some of the things that he was learning. He gave
her a copy of *Good News for Bad Days*, not so she
would change, but so she would understand the
process he was going through. At this writing,
communication between them has improved remarkably and there is talk of a possible reconciliation in the marriage. The jury is still out, but
Patrick's newly found compassion at least has
opened a door to mutual understanding and
forgiveness.

## 4. Compassion is the antitoxin of the soul.

These words of longshoreman and philosopher
Eric Hoffer highlight another aspect of this stage

of soulful living. Once you know that inner peace is your goal—and that of everyone—it becomes possible to let go of attitudes and behaviors that have kept you from experiencing peace.

Hoffer uses the word "antitoxin," which suggests that there is something poisonous, or toxic, about our attitudes. Ordinarily, we think of poisons as things from the outside that can kill us. We do not often reflect that the ideas and feelings inside us can be toxins that kill the life of the soul.

The Bible story of the fall of Adam and Eve gives us a lesson in how our attitudes can poison us and an entire world. The peaceful bliss of Eden was shattered when a single idea was planted in the heads of our first parents: *You shall be as gods.* Until that idea entered their awareness, Adam and Eve had walked in a blissful relationship with God. God was with them, and they were with God every step of the way. Once they surrendered to the idea that they themselves could be gods, and so be in charge of everything, they were elated—ecstatic, in fact. It sounded very good to them, and they decided to go for it.

Like so many things in life, it seemed like a good idea at the time. Enchanted with the idea of being on a par with God, Adam and Eve thought they were on top of the world. Soon, they realized that instead of expanding their horizons they had restricted them. Whereas before, they and God and nature had always been in harmony, now there was a rift in the relationship. Instead of being one with God and nature, now Adam and Eve had to appease both of them, to the point of treating natural forces as gods. God was displeased with them, and the forces of nature (the sun, the moon, and the earth) often worked against them. Once, the world had been a friendly place. They could no longer count on it being so.

In Paradise, they had never worried about the words "I can't" or "I want." With God at their side, there was plenty of everything, and there were no worries about their ability to get what they needed. Now, they had to earn their bread by the sweat of their brows (and by staying in the good graces of nature). Our first parents discovered that their energy was limited and that work was hard. They also discovered that, instead of there always being enough, their neighbors now wanted what they had. For the first time, Adam and Eve found themselves "having" (as they put it) to lie, to cheat, to steal, and even to kill if necessary in order to preserve what they had. Sorrow was rampant, too. Tragically, Adam and Eve had the sad duty of burying a son whom another son had murdered out of envy.

Being "as gods"—responsible for the entire universe—was not as wonderful an idea as it had seemed. The attitudes spawned by that one idea are the fruits of what we call "original sin." Unfortunately, those attitudes are very much alive in our world today. They still come from the basic and wrong idea that we can be gods, in charge of the world and accountable to no one. That one idea, passed down in the moral atmosphere from age to age, has done more to poison the morality of the world than any other thought or feeling in the history of humankind.

The antitoxin to the attitude that we are gods and accountable to no one is compassion. Hoffer is right. The word "compassion" means "to suffer with" in its Latin roots. Indeed, compassion is the very opposite of the arrogant insouciance of sin. Compassionate people have a feeling and an understanding for others. They may disagree vehemently with someone else's decision or course of action. But they understand that, however skewed or unreasonable or downright evil someone's actions may be, that person is somehow trying to find inner peace. There is no need to try to retaliate or "get the other guy," because they see no reason to be threatened by someone else's behavior toward them. The "logic" of sin does not apply.

Once, someone who had been working for me for a long time abruptly decided to quit, claiming that I had not been appreciative enough of him. Sad to say, there was a time in my life when I would have vociferously defended myself in such a situation, and even lashed out verbally against such charges. This time, I was pleased to find myself calmly saying that to my mind, his accusations were unwarranted. While I was sorry if anything I had done or said had hurt him, I recognized that behind his complaints, his soul was looking to move on to something else, and I respected that and wished him well. The difference in my response was compassion. I saw behind the veneer of his reasons for quitting, his soul's real desire to be doing something else. That freed me from being defensive so I could approach the situation with compassion and understanding. It detoxified a toxic situation.

It's the same with Patrick. Patrick loathed his wife's actions in leaving him for another man, but once he understood that in her own way she was looking for peace, he was able to bring compassion and understanding to his relationship with her. Whatever the outcome will be, Patrick's compassion has made the situation less toxic and much more peaceful.

## 5. Compassion opens the door to experiencing inner guidance.

The toxic nature of so much of the way we tend to think closes the door to our souls. When we are full of poison, our hearts and minds have precious little time or energy for anything but concentrating on how bad things are.

When we come to understand (but not necessarily to agree with) the thoughts and deeds of others, there is an amazing shift within ourselves. Suddenly it becomes clear to us that there is something beyond our judgment, our anger, our feelings of resentment. No longer do we find ourselves crippled by what others do or by our feelings about who they are or what they have done. We are our own person. Our happiness no longer depends upon what they do or whether we agree with them. We are free from all such considerations and especially of the need to change anyone else. From somewhere down within us, we are aware of our own inner drive for peace, and we know that for us, this inner drive will always be a source of guidance.

When Patrick is tempted to criticize his wife or especially to try to change her, he can remember that he is not defined as a success or a failure by her actions. He realizes that as long as he gives in to toxic thoughts he will increasingly cut himself off from the peace that he truly wants.

Note that in no way does this soulful sense of compassion imply the absence of an objective moral order. In fact, soulful compassion reveals that the very basis of moral order is found in the Golden Rule: "Do unto others as you would have them do unto you." The Golden Rule establishes that there are objective things that are right and wrong in our dealings with other people, and that we have a moral compass by which to judge that morality. Moreover, under the Golden Rule, you have every right to point out to someone what you believe to be right or wrong. Presumably, that would be one of the things you would want someone else to do for you. Compassion and mutual respect fuel the Golden Rule, which in turn fuels the objective moral order.

Though it sounds wonderful when you speak about it, compassion can be a very difficult road to trod. Jesus advised his followers to "follow the narrow road," and compassion is certainly an aspect of that narrow road. Though people tout the value of self-expression at all costs, compassion often demands restraint and respect for the other person. Apply the moral compass: do you really feel better when you unload your angry and negative feelings on another person? It often takes the full force of prudence and fortitude to refrain from delivering an angry outburst or a shattering retort. Compassion demands that you be that rare person who holds an angry tongue in check.

Compassion does not imply that we cannot be frank with someone with whom we have a legitimate issue. Holding our tongues when we should speak is sometimes not a virtue. A criticism, delivered with poise and compassion, will often do more than an angry outburst to bring home a point.

Having said that, it is important to note that soulful compassion demands that we not be excessively concerned about being "right." There are people who seem to care more about being right than they do about communicating the truth. In most disputes, both parties have a mixture of right and wrong in their points of view. I believe more marriages would be saved if spouses stopped telling each other who is right and who is wrong. It is possible to be very wrong while being very right. Patrick would still have the sixth commandment on his side if he were to verbally blast his wife for her affair, but it would not be the course that soulful compassion would demand. A better way of proceeding would be to say, "There is definitely a right and a wrong here. Let's work together to find it."

When that happens, the force of beauty that is at the innermost core of our souls can come out. That beauty is contagious. Where nervous rancor once charged the atmosphere, now compassion and mutual respect fill the air. It is like what Jane Austen once said of our knowledge of Shakespeare. "Shakespeare," she opined, "one gets acquainted with, without knowing how. . . . His thoughts and beauties are so spread abroad that one touches them everywhere; one is intimate with him by instinct."

Intimacy by instinct is the fruit of soulful compassion, which fills the atmosphere about us with beauty and peace. Recognizing that, we become intimate with it by instinct, and we learn how to be even more compassionate people. And so our compassion and its fruits become inner guides that lead us to want to make the sorts of decisions that will yield such sweet results.

Early in my radio career, I interviewed Gerald Jampolski and Diane Cirincione, a beautiful and caring couple whose books, workshops, and charitable actions bring life and love to millions around the world, especially to children. In one of our conversations, Gerald and Diane gave me the gift of a phrase that changed my life: "I can have peace instead of this." Remembering this phrase when a lack of compassion threatens to cloud our innermost environment reminds us to tap our inner resources of understanding and love instead. Remembering that what we truly want is peace charges the atmosphere around us with compassion and understanding. What do you know—this feels like what we truly want! Now we know more about how to direct ourselves in the future.

### 6. Compassion teaches you the meaning of the words "No matter what."

Once we have tasted compassion and felt its sweetness within our souls, we will do anything to keep it. I love the words of the early twentieth-century sociologist Charles Horton Conley: "No matter what a man does, he is not fully sane or fully human unless there is a spirit of freedom in him, a soul confined by purpose and larger than the practicable world." This spirit of freedom is bred of compassion, the deep inner understanding of what we want and what we are here for. Once you have savored the presence of beauty and peace in your soul, you want it no matter what. That is why I refused to argue with the man who wanted to move on from my employ. I wanted both him (if possible) and me (certainly) to experience peace, no matter what.

I hope it is clear to you that when I say "peace no matter what," it does not mean allowing yourself to suffer in silence while someone abuses you physically, spiritually, or psychologically. Nor does it mean being abusive in return. Soulful peace no matter what in the face of abuse means asking two questions:

1. *What must I do to stop or remove myself from this abusive behavior?*

2. *What must I do to ensure that I and everyone else in this situation experiences true peace?*

No matter what, I am committing myself to stopping the abuse and looking within for guidance as to how to heal and go on with life. On the one hand, you cannot allow the abuse to continue. You must remove yourself and help others to do the same insofar as that's possible. Plus, you don't want to deal with the situation by putting more abuse and toxicity into the world. No matter what, you must find the inner way to true beauty and peace and there find how to transform your hurt into grace, to move past the pain to live a life dedicated to peace in the world.

How do we do this? I take inspiration from one of the dearest and most inspiring human beings I have ever known, the late Professor Robert J. Kreyche of Rockhurst College and the University of Arizona at Tempe (UAT). Though I was never formally his student at Rockhurst, we became friends while I was still an undergraduate and after he had moved to Tempe. A philosopher's philosopher, Dr. Kreyche insisted in his writings and in his life that philosophy—even logic—had to be practical. Weekdays, he taught philosophy at UAT, and on weekends he taught and helped migrant workers and their families. One evening, on a visit to Kansas City, he unexpectedly stopped by my parents' house. I invited him into my room, and I can still see his lanky frame sitting in my chair as he, the professor, and I, the undergraduate, philosophized. I recall his saying to me that night something that he had written a decade before: "To know what is and to

adjust one's life to that knowledge is the highest
natural wisdom of man, a wisdom that inevitably
points the way to the source of all truth."

To know what is—that is the soul's first calling: to know what is in eternity and to know
what is here on earth. To adjust one's life to that
knowledge—that is the soul's second calling: to
bring eternity and daily life together in mutual
compassion and gracious action.

Soulful compassion opens for us a door to hear
the twofold calling of the soul within us. No
matter how painfully far we may have wandered
from eternity, compassion for ourselves and for
others can bring us back to the pursuit of our
long-lost ideals. No matter how far away we may
have strayed from the concerns of everyday people, compassion forms the bridge that helps us to
find our way back. No matter what, these eternal
things remain. No matter what, I am committed
to fostering them here on earth.

# Tapestry—Discerning a Pattern in the Pieces of Our Lives

Once you know the meaning of the words "no matter what," you are free to take a good look at your life. In the past, when you have looked at your life, you have found it wanting. You have blamed parents, siblings, friends, and enemies—even yourself—for offenses and mistakes. As you discover the world of soul, you look differently at the moments you once thought to be random and even destructive. You begin to see the possibility that the events of your life are threads that form a tapestry. Seeing your life as a tapestry can open your eyes to patterns and even a beauty you've never seen before. It can help you to assess what aspects of your life you want to keep and to discern the directions of future change.

There's a young homeless woman who sits in our church all day long. Over the year or so she has been doing this, Margaret has become progressively disoriented. When she first came to us, she would just sit quietly. Over the past several months, she has started talking to herself and occasionally becomes very angry, though never violent. Time and time again, we have talked to her, offered her help, treatment, and various kinds of programs. She will have none of them. Day after day she sits, leaving for the night, only to return when we open the church for the day.

It makes me sad to see Margaret, because she is so young and so full of promise. I have to remind myself that perhaps in some eternal plan, Margaret is fulfilling a role in the world. It is hard for me to see it, and it seems there could be so much more to her life.

I see Margaret, and I think of my friend Terry. Terry must be about the same age as Margaret, and indeed the two women have traveled similar paths. When I look at Terry now, it is hard for me to imagine that this beautiful, vivacious woman once raged and ranted through the streets, crazed and homeless. Who would guess that at one point her life seemed to be going nowhere?

Now a college graduate with a good position and formulating concrete plans for her life, Terry talks openly about her former days. "It was like spending endless days in a dark tunnel," she recalls. "I was in this bottomless sea of raging emotions, looking for a place to strike. I was drifting, churning about wildly, and getting nowhere."

What changed things for Terry? One day, in the streets, she met a Catholic nun who looked into her eyes and saw the spark of potential that we sometimes see in Margaret. Something about the sister drew Terry, and when the nun invited her home, Terry went with her.

"That nun was the greatest blessing in my life," Terry told me recently. "She took me in, made sure I was fed and clothed and washed. Then she got me to the doctor." After consid-

erable testing, the doctors were able to diagnose the medical condition behind Terry's behavior and to prescribe medication that would
help her.

"It was a revelation for me to realize that I
had a condition that could be named. I thought I
was the only one who was like that, that it was
me against the world. Now I could see that mental illness like mine was not so unusual, that others had it, too, and that by degrees it was
treatable. We who are its victims need not live in
fear and darkness forever."

Terry was lost and had fallen through the
cracks. She came to understand that she was not
alone and to feel understanding and compassion
for others like her.

Once she was seeing life in brighter colors and
with compassionate eyes, Terry felt the need to
make sense of her life. "I desperately needed for
those years of mental illness not to be lost years,"
she told me. "I needed to use them as a bench-
mark for the rest of my life."

In the period that followed, Terry made the
most of her new life, while continuing to try to
make sense of the old. She discovered that there
were some truly humiliating and embarrassing

moments. Of course, she was tempted to put them aside and to force them from her memory. "I finally realized that those horrible moments could be doorways to love," she told me. "They would remind me of what it was like to be crazy, and they gave me the signs I needed to determine whether I was having a relapse, needed to adjust my medication or diet or sleep schedule. Instead of being moments of pure horror, they became teachers and guides that kept me on course."

Terry also learned that deep within her lay a solid core of discipline. As she looked beneath the turmoil of her emotions, she discovered that she could be hardworking and responsible, even under very difficult conditions.

Reflecting on her years of illness, Terry learned that there were pockets of love in her life. Through the ups and downs, her parents had been deeply supportive of her. She determined to let them know what had been going on during those dark years. She promised that she would do everything in her power to return to them the steadfast love they had shown her.

As she rebuilt her life, Terry found herself being drawn to a dynamic Roman Catholic church in her city, one that had a warm community who made her feel welcome from the moment she walked in the door. She began to explore the new family she was finding there, and found a special friend in the priest who was the pastor. At about the same time, she met me in a Catholic chat room online. After she assured herself that I was a "real priest," we became friends. It is a privilege to watch her courageous growth and to share in the ups and downs of it. Eventually, Terry began the process of becoming a formal member of the Catholic Church. Her family was not happy about this idea, since they had had bad experiences with the Church and therefore had some understandably harsh feelings about Catholics. Yet their support for her was unwavering.

Terry discovered that in her new world there was a lot of love to count on. This gave her the strength to face some memories that were harder to heal. She discovered some friends and family members who had distanced themselves and even walked away because of her past erratic behavior. Instead of hating them in return, she came to understand their reactions and determined to do what she could to make amends.

As her sense of worth and personal value grew in the supportive atmosphere around her, Terry began to contemplate a new direction in her life. She experienced a deep inner desire to return to the world something of what she had been given. At present, she has a good new job and is looking at concrete options for a career of service.

What has happened to Terry? She has reflected on her life, looked at the individual pieces of it, and allowed them to weave themselves into a tapestry of love and service.

*✍*

There are several things that you learn as you go through the tapestry stage.

1. *The events in our lives are not mere coincidence.*

2. *The moments of our lives, even the painful ones, are teachers and guides.*

3. As we take stock of our lives, we can begin to draw people to ourselves who are empathetic to our new purpose.

4. As we review our life, we learn to see it as a tapestry rather than as a series of unconnected moments. The expectation of meaning replaces the expectation of meaninglessness.

5. This expectation of a tapestry helps us to gradually replace the notion of life as fickle with the notion that life is something we can count on.

## 1. The events in our lives are not mere coincidence.

The Buddhists say, "When the student is ready, the teacher will appear." I think the insight that the events in our lives are not mere coincidences is one that surfaces when we are ready to discern the tapestry of our lives. Until then, we might say that we are victims of good luck or bad luck, or we might smile tolerantly when someone says that our lives are not merely coincidental. It generally takes some time before we are ready to see that there are patterns to happenings and that we can do something to change those patterns if we wish.

I was well into adulthood before I thought very much about all this. I had spent considerable time in religious training and had been in therapy. I was certainly familiar with the data from my past. One of the oddest things I have learned is that so often our religious training and experience can coincide with immature attitudes and painfully inadequate notions about life. Religion can help us come to awareness, but being religious does not guarantee that we will. It's the same with therapy. It can leave us profoundly knowledgeable about our past, yet still feeling as though we are its victims.

I first began to take seriously the notion that life is not coincidental after I had been hosting "As You Think" for about three years. I had interviewed Wayne Dyer, Marianne Williamson, and Thomas Moore and read a great deal of the spirituality of the day. I left my parish one afternoon and on the way to the radio station, I ran into a parishioner who had been having some personal difficulties, but whom I had not seen for quite some time. I remember being amazed at meeting this person whom I had just been thinking about. We finished our conversation and I went on to the station to tape an interview with an author. During the interview, I was amazed to realize that, on the heels of this "chance encounter," I was interviewing James and Salle Redfield about *The Celestine Prophecy*, a central tenet of which is that there are no coincidences!

That experience propelled me across the threshold of discovering that my life was a tapestry, not a bunch of disconnected threads thrown into a basket. Now I could see that there was a pattern behind my childhood love of radio and desire for the priesthood, my years of discouragement and depression, my illness and unexpected recovery, and reorientation into radio and priesthood. All of them were part of an overall purpose.

That is what Terry discovered about her life; as it had done for me, this discovery freed her to accept and to create a whole new identity and to see new dimensions in the world.

$\mathscr{L}$

## 2. The moments of our lives, even the painful ones, are teachers and guides.

Ron was in his early fifties when he came to see me. He was wrestling with issues of self-respect and had come to question whether he was making any contribution at all to the world.

"I'll never forget the day my father told me that I was useless," he recounted. "I was eight or nine years old. I don't remember exactly what happened to trigger the incident, but I remember my father standing angrily before me, saying, 'Young man, it's about time you started to make a contribution to this family. All you do is take, take, take. You never think of anyone but yourself.' Looking back, it seems like a remarkable thing to say to an eight-year-old, but of course I didn't know that at the time. I believed him. I came to believe that I was not contributing a single thing to my family."

That was bad enough. What made matters worse was another incident, a recent one, that bore an ironic similarity to the incident from childhood. "Getting this job," Ron told me, "was like a miracle. I had been sick and unable to work for about a year. It meant everything to me, and I was starting to feel like I was doing something important.

"About three weeks ago, we had a visit from one of the vice presidents from the corporate headquarters. He and I had a pleasant chat, and he seemed happy with my work. Imagine my surprise to get a letter from this executive today, telling me that I was draining more from the company than I was giving, and that this situation would not be tolerated. I am devastated. I am so angry, I feel like telling them what they can do with their job."

What Ron really wanted, beneath the hurt and frustration, was not another job, but rather a sense of peace—in his case, a sense of making a genuine contribution. It made it easier that he himself discerned the similarity between the childhood incident and the recent one. That made it less difficult for him to face the real question: into what pattern was he going to weave the threads? Was he going to weave them into a tapestry in which he was the defeated victim of people more powerful than he who didn't appreciate him? Or was he going to weave them into a pattern in which he would get the peace and satisfaction he really desired? If he did the former, he might angrily resign or sulk in silence. If he did the latter, he might win the boss over, or he might hang tough and take measures to make his contributions to the firm better known. Or he might do both of these things while looking for other work.

In any event, his decision will hinge upon his awareness that there is some meaning to the events of his life and how positively or negatively he assesses that meaning. Ron has learned the importance of allowing the moments of his life to teach him and to guide him, rather than simply reacting to them.

### 3. As we take stock of our lives, we begin to draw people unto ourselves who are empathetic to our new purpose.

As Terry learned to allow the past to teach and guide her, she began to find people at work and at church who supported the soulful changes she was making. Her newfound compassion and understanding drew people who were empathetic with her goals and directions and who would

help her. When people came along who were
unhelpful, she learned that meeting them was
often a step toward meeting just the people she
needed. For example, in the course of looking for
a more meaningful line of work, she interviewed
at an office where she was treated very unkindly
about her background and her life. When I heard
from Terry after the incident, there was almost
no talking to her, she was so angry. After she had
had a few days to vent her feelings, a measure of
hope dawned from deep within her. She realized
that she did not want to let her bad experience
keep her from pursuing what she really wanted to
do with her life. She then went on to other inter-
views and experienced a warm and enthusiastic
acceptance. It seems that the first experience chal-
lenged and tested her desire and led her to discover that it was real and worth pursuing.

Experience, they say, is the best teacher. Terry
took her bad experience and allowed it to propel
her toward her mission.

We see something similar with Ron. As he
became more aware of the destructive pattern of
criticism in his life, he was eventually able to
remove the scars of his father's insensitive and
harsh remarks and to distance himself from the

equally insensitive remarks of his superior. Whether he chooses to stay with the firm or not, Ron will now have a better class of thoughts by which to guide his life. I am sure that his mentors from now on will prove to be more positive as well.

"Give me a lever," Archimedes said, "and I will move the world." The soul is a powerful lever. Once we allow it to sift out the wheat from the chaff in our lives, the soul moves our world to remake it. Like a magnet, the soul begins to draw better energy to itself, and therefore draws people who are more helpful to us in the pursuit of our journey. Once we allow the soul to be our ally, rather than ignoring it or resisting it, it shows us new people and new things—new clues. Once I decided to work in radio, I found myself meeting the engineer who introduced me to the radio account executive who became my producer. Before I knew it, I was doing two shows and working full-time in radio ministry.

That doesn't mean that everything was rosy. Along the way, I was also in the company of some people who would have loved to see my work destroyed. I have often wondered why they were in my life. I believe their presence was my soul's way of testing me to see whether I was really serious about following its call to radio ministry. So were the long years of scraping and struggling to raise the money for "As You Think." The soul offers us life-renewing challenges and tests our mettle as we respond to them.

4. As we review our life, we learn to see it as a tapestry rather than as a series of unconnected moments. The expectation of meaning replaces the expectation of meaninglessness.

As we become comfortable with the fact that the events of life happen for a reason, there develops a subtle shift in our consciousness, which, in turn, has an effect upon our lives. Where once we believed and expected that our lives were a matter of one random occurrence after another, now we find ourselves beginning to look for a meaning and purpose behind these events. Realizing this and coming to expect it, we start to feel less like victims. Instead, we look to our experiences for signs and indications as to where we are going in life.

Some time ago, a bizarre and unpleasant confrontation with a friend led me to the realization that it was no longer a good idea to continue the relationship. Like most of us, I am loathe to make such decisions about people I care about, and for some time I had been trying to maintain the friendship despite grave reservations and considerable stress. At length, the pivotal incident occurred which led me to believe that it was time to bid this person farewell. I made the decision, all the while feeling absolutely awful. At the same time, I believed deep down that my decision was really a good one.

While all this was going on, I began to notice something else taking place in my life. I began to receive messages and expressions of love and affirmation from friends and acquaintances in enormous waves of abundance. I sat in amazement as letters, notes, cards, phone calls, conversations, and gifts swirled around me, telling me how much and how deeply I was loved. By then, I was firmly established in my belief that nothing happened by coincidence; it was that belief that led me to have faith in my decision about my friend. It was also that belief—honed into an expectation—that helped me not to miss what was happening in this April shower of affection that I was experiencing. These people had no idea of what I was going through; by and large they didn't even know of each other's existence. I saw that God was telling me that I was not alone and would have an abundance of help and love in the wake of my difficult decision.

One evening, as all of this was taking place, I boarded a crowded commuter train to ride back to the city from an outing. I was dreading the trip, fearing that I would spend the time churning over the recent unpleasant events in my mind. I took the precaution of grabbing a religious magazine from a pamphlet rack in the station, hoping that reading it would distract me from my worries.

The train was exceptionally packed that night, and I wondered if I would be able to find a seat. As I boarded the train, I turned left and took the first aisle seat I could find. As I sat down, I noticed to my immediate left a young woman holding two of the cutest little white dogs I had ever seen. Their bright button eyes peeked out from the curly white fur of their adorable little faces with wonder and amazement at this new passenger who had joined them. The young woman began to apologize but I assured her that I loved animals and they were no problem. I asked their names (Trixie and Roxy), their breed (Maltese), and their age (nine). Thus began a fascinating conversation with an intelligent and vivacious lawyer who spent considerable time doing volunteer work for organizations involved in rescuing abused animals. As we talked, I stroked Trixie's and Roxy's little heads. Before long, Roxy, reputed to be reserved, was eagerly licking my hand. Between the 125th Street and Grand Central stations, Trixie crawled into my lap and happily nuzzled me and accepted kisses. When I said good-bye to my traveling companions and headed home, I realized that God had wonderfully taken care of my potentially anxious train ride.

When we come to know that the events of our lives are neither random nor meaningless, we can begin to treat them as messengers. With all of the interest in angels today, I wish that more of us might come to see our experiences as angels—messengers from God that reveal to us the wonderful treasure that we are and how deeply we are cared for and loved. At the tapestry soul stage, we may not yet have a full-blown realization of God and his ways of working in our lives. What we do have is the sense that our lives are not random and that we can expect our experiences to have messages for us to guide us on our way.

As I was writing these words, the morning mail arrived with a letter from my friend Mary Barletti. She and her husband, Joe, have become friends over the years, and I always look forward to seeing them or hearing from them. Mary was writing to thank me for a retreat I gave for married couples at the Passionist Spiritual Center in Riverdale, New York. In the course of her letter, Mary mentioned the reflections I had shared about the wedding feast at Cana, the gospel story in which Jesus changes water into wine. Reading Mary's letter, I realized that, without consciously intending to, she had given me the Bible story I needed to illustrate my point about messages. What a coincidence! Oops.

The story of the wedding feast at Cana, which is found in the second chapter of the Gospel according to St. John in the New Testament, is generally treated as a story of Jesus changing water into wine when the wine ran out at a wedding. Scripture scholars know that its significance is much deeper theologically than that popular summary would lead us to suspect. From the point of view of tapestry, the story shows us how life events are not as random as they might appear to be on the surface, and helps us to see the importance of setting our expectations in the direction of meaning.

St. John reports that Mary, the mother of Jesus, was present at the wedding and tells us that Jesus and his disciples "had also been invited." Those words are striking, because they represent the manner in which we often do things. There's always a little irony in John's gospel, and he is subtly telling us that the great prophet and Son of God was something of an afterthought (also invited) among the guests at the wedding. St. John is reminding us that we often try to do things by ourselves, with God as a kind of after-thought. When they did that at the wedding, the wine ran out. For us, too, when we do things our own way, barely remembering to "invite" God into our activities, we often find that the "wine" —the joy, the élan, the energy in our daily achievements—runs out. We are left wondering why we have not had more success or more joy in our lives and our achievements.

When that happens, as we have been observ-ing, we feel the "dis-ease" in our souls. I don't think it would be too far-fetched to say that in this story, Mary represents the soul—that aspect of us that bridges the temporal and the eternal. In the story, she takes the utterly lost (stage 1) situation of the newly married couple and brings it to Jesus: "They have no wine." The newlyweds have fallen through the cracks and are humiliated (stage 2). Notice that it is Mary's compassion (stage 3) that bridges the encounter of the hopeless human situation with the hope of the eternal and divine.

The resolution is not immediate, however. Invited as an afterthought, Jesus—representing the eternal dimension of reality—reacts as a second-choice guest might well react. He says to his mother, "What is it to me and to thee?" If this seems like a horrible response from the representative of the eternal, realize why he makes it. In order for our lives to be righted, we must break through the illusion that we can go it alone and instead must come to the understanding that our temporal lives are charged with the grandeur of an eternal destiny, which we must allow to capture our attention.

I'm sure that at this point in the story, the young couple threw their hands up in despair (as do we, when God doesn't seem to answer our prayers immediately). At such moments, the soul (Mary, here) forces the issue, turning the hopeless temporal matter over to eternity. Turning to the couple's servants, Mary says to them, "Do whatever He tells you." When she says that—and when we allow our souls to do the same thing in our hopelessness—the miracle can happen and the last wine (circumstances) is better than the first. Our soul's, like Mary's, expectancy that meaning will replace meaninglessness allows God to make the new wine flow. Terry and Ron and I will tell you so.

**5. This expectation of a tapestry helps us to gradually replace the notion of life as fickle with the notion that life is something we can count on.**

The final hallmark of the tapestry stage is that the presence of the divine itself is not taken to be yet another coincidence, but rather becomes our understanding and our expectation. Unlike the proverbial "Hail Mary" pass where we throw up a prayer and hope that God answers it, the tapestry stage leads us to a soulfulness that knows and expects that the ways of God are involved in our ways and are wiser and better. When we expect this kind of care from God, we look upon our lives differently. Instead of looking to them as malicious or dead events, we now look behind them for the handwriting of God.

During the writing of this chapter, I had the privilege of being interviewed on a radio program called "Strategies for Living" on KFLO in Shreveport, Louisiana. The host of the show, Dave McMillan, read a story a listener had E-mailed to him. It was called "God's Handiwork." The author of the story recalled a time when, as a young boy, he looked at some needlework his mother was doing. He was disappointed because she was using dark threads and the pattern she was sewing looked ugly. When her son complained about her handiwork, the mother told him to go off and play, and promised to call him back when she was finished. The author recalled how surprised he was when his mother called him over to see the finished product. It was beautiful.

"How did you get something so beautiful out of something so ugly?" the boy inquired, truly puzzled.

"Son," his mother said, "what you saw earlier was the bottom of the design. That's why it looked so ugly to you. While I was sewing, I was using a pattern—go find it there on the top of the box."

The boy ran and found the box, and saw the pattern his mother had been using. He brought it back and saw that by following the pattern, she had made something beautiful, even though in the making it looked haphazard and unattractive.

The soul stage of tapestry reminds us that when life seems random and ugly, oftentimes we are looking at the bottom of the design. It is the work of the soul to help us see the eternal pattern, and to follow that pattern toward the realization of a beautiful handiwork.

STAGE FIVE

# *Attic Wisdom—Becoming at Home With the Eternal*

The realization that your life is more than discontinuous strands of happenings opens you to a whole new horizon of living. That's what happened to Ann, who, in her mid-fifties, met the man of her dreams. Until then, Ann's love life, though extremely successful in many ways, had been a string of good relationships, none of which managed to end in marriage. Ann could not help wondering whether this pattern would ever end. She really wanted to find someone who would be a loving husband, for whom she would be a loving wife.

At length, she subscribed to an on-line service designed to help people meet other eligible people. After a couple of obvious ringers, she got the name of a man her age who seemed to have many of the qualities she desired in a partner. After corresponding for several months, and talking on the telephone, they nervously agreed to meet one weekend. Todd flew to Chicago where Ann lived. They met in public places, went to her church, and enjoyed the various tourist attractions of the Windy City. Each discovered in the other the warm, deeply religious, caring, romantic person they had been dreaming of. Though it was not immediately clear to them in what direction the relationship would go, it was clear to them that a higher force had brought them together.

Since both Ann and Todd were religious people, they were able to name that higher force as God. Alone and together, they began to develop a new relationship with God as the one who had brought them together and as the one whose love was something deeper and more central than they had ever imagined.

Ann and Todd were Christians, and as such had a particular frame of reference for this new experience of the divine. Had they been Buddhists, they might have experienced an overriding peace that would have contextualized their experience of life. Had they been Hindus, they might have experienced a peaceful gap or void that clearly framed the other moments of their lives.

However we experience the transcendent in our lives, when we do, it provides us with an entry into an entirely new dimension of being. Even if we have been religious before, we are religious now in a whole new way.

That was the experience of Tobit and his family in the Bible. The Book of Tobit is a hidden treasure of ancient wisdom. The original text of the book is no longer extant; it is not included in the Hebrew Bible and is in Protestant Bibles only as Apocrypha. Yet the text has strong Semitic origins and the story is powerful in and of itself as a tale of how the soul learns to live and move in God.

The ancient story of Tobit is full of intriguing twists and turns and is best appreciated through actual reading. The basic story is that Tobit, a kind and law-abiding man, is blinded due to a freak mishap. Because he is disabled, he cannot work; and so his wife, Anna, has to support them by spinning wool and weaving cloth. She is so successful that she receives a kid goat as a bonus for her work. When she brings the goat home, its bleating annoys Tobit, who accuses her of stealing the goat and tells her to get rid of it. In what amounts to a biblical account of a husband and wife having a fight, Anna angrily questions Tobit's virtue.

Worn down by the sheer weight of his life, Tobit offers a heartfelt prayer that God will let him die.

Meanwhile, in far-off Media, there lies a young woman named Sarah, whose seven husbands have all died. When her maid makes a disparaging comment about her marital misfortunes, Sarah falls apart and she, too, prays to God for death.

God hears these two desperate prayers which are simultaneously offered to him from diverse corners of the world. He determines to answer them and dispatches the angel Raphael to do so.

Confident that his prayer for death will be answered, Tobit sends his son Tobias to retrieve money he has left in Media. Raphael, disguised as a stranger, guides Tobias to go in pursuit of Sarah's hand. Tobias casts out the demon that has plagued Sarah's marital history and takes her for his wife. The couple then returns to Tobit and, with gall from a fish, Tobias cures his father's blindness. Tobit, his sight fully restored, praises God for his great blessings.

As I say, it is a magical story, one that merits a full reading. What moves me so much about the story is its emphasis upon the power of God to heal desperate conditions from diverse parts of the world through intertwining the stories of people who, at the outset, do not know each other.

Tobit's prayer toward the end of the story makes it explicit that his soul has risen to a new level of insight, symbolized by his physical sight being restored.

"He is our Master," Tobit says, "and He is our God, and He is our Father, and He is God forever and ever." (Tob. 13:4)

❧

The fifth stage of the soul is one at which the soul breaks through to the explicit knowledge of God. Increasingly along its journey, the soul has been moving farther away from the limitations imposed on it by the temporal world. Now it breaks through into the realm of the eternal and divine. What Tobit experienced, what Ann and Todd are experiencing, is a breakthrough, an insight into the other pole for which the soul was made—the eternal.

What happens to the soul at this stage is very much like climbing up into the attic of your house. That is why I call it "attic wisdom."

I can't recall ever having lived in a house with an attic, but I know many people who have. The fact that I have lived over five decades without an attic says a great deal about the architecture and style of our society. There used to be an attic in everybody's house. I almost said that attics were ordinary, but they were far from that. Attics were truly *extra*ordinary, magical places where dead things came to life and transformed us in the process.

Attics are sources of stories and family lore. I know a family whose spacious house has an attic. I have never been there, but my imagination has traveled there often. My friends talk about their attic as if it were an old family friend. When, from time to time, the phone lines malfunction, they say that the wires have become crossed in the attic. What elves crossed them is anybody's guess. When the telephone repairman comes, they have to open the trapdoor and let him roam about to untangle the mess the lines have become. Mind you, of the seven members of this family, only Mom and Dad (mostly Dad) have actually gone up to the attic. But everyone knows how the phone man has to climb up there whenever the lines get crossed. The attic contains magic, a mythology and a life of its own, and an important place in the family legend.

That attic, I hear, is the source of many treasures. Before fishing trips and family outings, coolers and scores of suitcases emerge from its lofty heights. At Christmastime, a dozen enormous cases are laboriously brought down the ladder. Those boxes contain dormant magic. Once opened, the magic awakens; in the wink of an eye, a once-bare Christmas tree is alive with lights and ornaments and memories, and the whole house—indoors and out—is blessed with the decor of Christmas. At holiday's end, back go the cases and the memories for another year.

Attics are wonderful places to visit. A rainy play day can be transformed into a joyous adventure by a climb up the stairs to the attic. In an attic we can tolerate a dankness and mustiness that are intolerable downstairs. Open a trunk—lo, there is Grandmother's wedding dress. A little girl on a free afternoon finds herself transformed into a bride and dances at her imaginary wedding. Oh, look—there are the old love letters Dad wrote to Mother when they were courting. A teenage daughter finds herself enraptured as she gains a whole new insight into her mother and dad and educates her heart as well. Rummaging through a rusty old tackle box, Dad finds the lure with which he caught his first fish on a fishing trip with his dad years ago. On a blustery winter's day, Junior and his teenage pals gather to listen to music and talk about adventures real and imagined. The attic provides a warm world insulated from the chill winds.

Why do we love attics so? We love them because they create a snug and magical world where we can go when our everyday world below becomes dull or too difficult. Even if we do not actually venture there, the mere thought of the attic transports us to that world, transforms us with that magic. Sherlock Holmes, master detective that he was, knew that attics and the human mind were kindred spirits. "I consider," remarked the inhabitant of 21B Baker Street, "that a man's brain is like a little empty attic, and you have to stock it with such furniture as you choose." Holmes was right—attics are so dear to us because they help us to furnish (warmly and nostalgically) the attics that lie just above our eyes!

Attics are special. They are different from basements, which bring us close to the earth. Wine cellars are basements in which Bacchus is brought to earth. Attics, instead, transport us to the heavens. Playing in the attic, we find ourselves reveling in timelessness: our present becomes the past, while at the same time we encounter our present as the future of our past. We become eternal.

Through attics, we become transcendent. Imaginatively or really, we open the door to the attic and pull down the stairs when our daily lives need something, lack something, want something. Did you know that in ancient times the word "transcend" meant "to climb"? When you climb the ladder to enter your attic, you are climbing out of your everyday world, with its burdens, routines, joys, mishaps, its whole and broken relationships, and are climbing to a loftier place to find a little magic.

That is the beauty of transcendence—it enables us to climb above the rough-and-tumble of everyday life in order to get some refreshment, a new sense of time and life.

Often we speak of transcendence as a necessity ("I *must* go to church or take a day off.") or as a wish contrary to fact ("I know I really *need* a day off, but who has time?"). More basically, however, transcendence is an invitation, a call. Just as an attic beckons to us on a rainy day, so there is a call within ourselves to simply climb away to something different, something more important than the daily grind. Not long ago, I realized that I had been working seven days a week for months. I could feel it in my bones. I love my work—that was not an issue—but something in my soul felt closed in, confined. I needed to get out from under the constant pressure of work, the constant rushing here and there to lead a service or to give a talk or attend a meeting. I felt as if I would scream if one more person scheduled another meeting or talk for me. I had to get to the attic.

How I got there is an interesting lesson in listening to the calls we hear within us. A Labor Day weekend loomed ahead. Generally, between services and radio programs, it is hard for me to get a weekend off. The Monday before the long weekend, someone from the radio station called to say that a football game would preempt "As You Think" on Saturday night. Sunday morning was free, radiowise, since I was not scheduled for "Religion on the Line." On Tuesday, I happened to mention to Father Daly at Our Lady of Peace that I didn't have any radio programs the following weekend. "Well," he said, "Why don't you take the weekend off? We can easily cover your Masses." Okay!

Now I had the time, but what would I do with it? I thought a lot about it and just told God, "Lord, you gave me this time. Show me what you want me to do." Wednesday, Thursday, Friday came. Still nothing emerged. I waited to see what would happen. Late Friday afternoon, two phone calls yielded two invitations! From a time stand-

point, I could really accept only one; so I had not
only one invitation but also an extra!

As things worked out, the weekend gave me
just the right amount of time at home to clean, to
read, and to play with my cats. It gave me delightful hours with friends whom I had not seen in a
long time. What is more, I had a lot of time to
think and to pray, especially about my work
schedule and about what was important in life.

Labor Day proved even more interesting.
Around noon, a friend called and suggested we
have lunch at a restaurant in Hoboken that we
both know and like. We drove there, only to find
the restaurant closed for the holiday. In an adven-
turous mood, we decided to drive ninety min-
utes to a restaurant in Westport, Connecticut. We
did, only to find that place closed as well. "Third
time's the charm," we said, and made our way to
Norwalk to yet another place. On the way, the
heavens burst open with a powerful storm that
knocked down trees and drenched the country-
side. We made it to the restaurant—and, yes, the
place was open. But how to get from the parking
lot to the restaurant without getting soaked?

As if by magic, there appeared a man carrying
an enormous umbrella, running from the restau-

rant to the car parked next to us. We rolled down the window and asked if we could borrow his umbrella to get to the restaurant. "Sure," he said. "Just give it to the red-haired lady at the door." Not only did we have dry passage to the restaurant, we were able to transport the umbrella back to its rightful owner. Once inside, we enjoyed a delightful lunch in a country inn, with classical music and a view of the rain. I could not have planned it any better myself.

What I am describing, I know, is an unusual view of transcendence. We normally think of transcendence as going away on retreat, or spending long hours meditating, or thinking lofty thoughts. Indeed, these are valid forms of transcendence. But, fundamentally, transcendence means placing ourselves in whatever situation allows us to climb beyond our present lives and into the attic of our soul.

Once there, we find a very special relationship with time. A little girl, finding her mother's prom dress, becomes both old and young. Attic Standard Time is past, present, and future all in one.

Our souls beg us to transcend. They cry when we immerse them too long and too much in our routines, just as I had done in the weeks before

Labor Day. We can trust our souls to know what is best. As I learned on that Labor Day weekend, our souls know precisely what to do with their trip to the attic once we agree to put our feet on the stairs.

However, once they have had their romp upstairs, our souls bid us to return. That is the funny thing about souls—they love to play in the heights, but they are truly at home only when they come back down to earth. That is an old bit of wisdom. Twenty-five hundred years ago, Plato told the world about a cave in which people were chained to the wall. One of them broke loose and, leaving the cave, discovered the light of truth. After spending enlightened time contemplating the world of ideas, he returned to the cave in order to share his experience with the others.

Plato's enlightened one from millennia gone by resonates in the souls of people we know. The times in which we are pulled away from what is familiar to us can become times of great insight, which in turn can lead us into a new presence in the world. Linda, a successful businesswoman who became disabled, now dreams of working with disabled children. Mothers Against Drunk Driving was formed by parents incensed by a light sentence given to a repeat offender whose inebriated driving caused the death of a teenage girl. A former radio guest of mine, Mary Jane Cathers, founded Triune to help brain-damaged people, after having sustained a brain injury herself. Christians remember that before going to the cross, Jesus went to the upper room to celebrate the Last Supper. With its infinite variety of scenarios, life demands that we pull away from the details to play in the universals and then sends us back into the world with a new mission and presence.

It is a pity that more houses don't have attics these days. We need the upper rooms in our lives to take us away from our everyday existence with its often-crippling limitations. We need our attics in order that we might be transformed into people of inspiration and mission, people ready to make a difference in the world. We need our attics. It is an act of grace that they beckon to us and call us to imagination, rapture, and hope.

*L*

What is it, then, that we experience when our souls cross the threshold into the realm of the eternal or transcendent, into their attic? The priest-poet Gerard Manley Hopkins found that "Christ plays in ten thousand places," and there are at least that many ways in which to designate the eternal.

If we are artists, we might think of eternal beauty and its three qualities so magnificently named by Thomas Aquinas—integrity (wholeness), consonance (every part contributing to the tone of the piece), and clarity (brilliance, luminosity, and accessibility to the soul)—and might make those three qualities the objects of our attention and our focus.

If we are philosophers, we might focus our attention upon eternal qualities such as beauty, truth, and goodness. Or, if we are looking for the eternal in our moral lives, we might choose the cardinal virtues: prudence, justice, fortitude, and temperance.

If we are harried citizens of the everyday world, we might find ourselves gazing more and more on the nature of peace.

If we are like Ann and Todd, we might find ourselves gazing soft-eyed at the nature of love.

There are many ways—ten thousand and more—to access the eternal.

And behind it all, there is God. Christians, Jews, and Moslems call him the Supreme Being. Hindus call him the Void. Buddhists don't speak of God, but speak of nirvana, a state of ultimate bliss. All of us are trying to use the name of that which is beyond everything that we can know or experience or name. Mark Twain captured something of our dilemma in trying to name God when he said, "India has two million gods, and worships them all. In religion other countries are paupers; India is the only millionaire." And Montaigne described it in another way when he wrote, "Oh senseless man, who cannot possibly make a worm, and yet will make Gods by dozens."

Jesus called God "Father" and encouraged his disciples, lost and frightened on the night before he died, "Trust in God still, and trust in me." (John 14:1)

The joy of the fifth stage of the soul is a joy that is mixed with struggle and is sometimes overwhelmed by what it is trying to do. At this soul stage, we are learning to cast off the chains that daily bind us as they bound Plato's prisoners, and we are learning to contemplate what is eternal and most real. "The mind," said the American poet James Russell Lowell, "can weave itself warmly in the cocoon of its own thoughts, and dwell a hermit anywhere." In the attics of our souls, we experience the freedom and the playfulness that is the hallmark of those who know how to come home to the eternal.

If you want to know what to do once the bug of the eternal has bitten you, turn to the psalms. There you will find the soul weaving warmly its cocoon as it dwells upon the eternal. "God, hear my cry for help, listen to my prayer" (Ps. 61); "Give thanks to the Lord, for he is good, his love is everlasting" (Ps. 107); "Lord, you probe me and you know me, you know if I am standing or sitting, you read my thoughts from far away" (Ps. 139). As you read these verses, think of yourself as a child playing in an attic, trying on this hat or that coat, unearthing that old picture or love letter, learning to breathe in the rarefied atmosphere of the eternal. On unhappy days, there is Psalm 137: "Out of the depths I cry to you, O Lord; Lord, hear my voice." On scary days, Psalm 140: "Lord, rescue me from evil people; defend me from violent men." Of a weary evening, try Psalm 141: "My prayers rise like incense, my hands like the evening offering." At a time of loss, Psalm 23: "Even though I walk in the valley of the shadow of death, I fear no evil; for you are at my side." The psalms are like that old trunk in the attic, full of treasures, with a surprise for every occasion.

Attic wisdom teaches us many things about ourselves, our world, and life.

1. *Our souls call and lead us beyond the threshold of the temporal into the world of the eternal.*

2. *There are myriad ways to access the eternal.*

3. *We are called to look beyond the tapestry of our life for the one who is weaving it.*

4. *In the attic of our soul we have the ability to "dwell a hermit" in any situation.*

5. *You can do it. Attic wisdom is as much for you as it is for a monk in a monastery.*

**1. Our souls call and lead us beyond the threshold of the temporal into the world of the eternal.**

Behind everything that we look for or think we want in the temporal world, there lies something abstract that defines it or gives it its essence. This is the soul stage at which we discover that directly. For it is here that we get in touch with what is behind everything that we experience or think we want, and what is behind the tapestry our lives have formed. Now, we are looking to the essence of what we seek. In fact, we are looking for the very essence of reality.

This fifth soul stage is a significant step in our maturity. Most of us spend a great deal of our lives wanting things without knowing why we

want them. We want a spouse. We want a big
house. We want a good and lucrative career. We
want a lot of money. Many times, we get all of
these, or most of them, and still find ourselves
needy and unhappy. What we need to do, instead,
is to ask ourselves, "What is the essence of what
I want?" Perhaps I want security. Perhaps I want
love. Perhaps I want to feel important. There is
always a reason that we want what we want, and
our soul begs us to stretch to the point of asking
what that reason is.

Then comes the second step: asking whether
the reason I have picked should really be the reason that drives my life. For example, if I'm honest enough to admit that I want a lot of money
because money makes me feel important, I might
find myself noticing something in the paper about
somebody my age who died, leaving behind a lot
of money and importance. That might get me
wondering whether money and importance are
really things that I should center my life around.
That is just the sort of reflection that can hurl me
across the threshold of the fifth soul stage, leading me to look at what is really eternal and really
lasting as a value for my life.

2. **There are myriad ways to access the eternal.**

At a time of crisis in their lives, people will often turn to works of philosophy and theology that they haven't looked at since college days, or they will turn to serious literature or to religion. There, they find a way of grappling with the things that are really lasting. As we have seen, there are a number of ways of naming the ideals. They all come down to the same questions. What is truly real? Have I been devoting myself to things that are silly, fleeting, and useless? Could I do better, and how can I know how to do better? Then comes the focus on beauty, truth, and goodness; the Seven Gifts of the Holy Spirit; or other ways of naming the things that last. At some point, there will arise the question of God, the question of how the ideals and virtues and values got there.

When I was just starting as a college teacher, an also-young but more experienced teacher happened to mention to me Dietrich Bonhoeffer's *Letters and Papers from Prison*. I have never forgotten Bonhoeffer's treatment of life as polyphonic music—how we seek to find the one note that will harmonize all of the other notes in our lives. I think that in prison, Bonhoeffer was in his attic, looking to make sense of life in the face of horrendous injustice, looking to find God in the grim reality of the 1930s and 1940s. Another prisoner by the name of Viktor Frankl at the very same moment was seeking to find meaning in the treachery that was being visited upon his people. He came up with a quote from Nietzsche: "Anyone with a why to live for can put up with almost any how." Eternity can come to us anywhere and in myriad ways, often in the wake of tragedy.

## 3. We are called to look beyond the tapestry of our life for the one who is weaving it.

Whenever I talk to married couples or advise them, I find myself shying away from communications skills or psychological techniques. By and large, I find myself leading them into a conversation about spirituality, about God. That doesn't mean we ignore their problems, mistakes, sins, and failures, or that we don't at some point talk about skills that would help them overcome these things. It means that we have to get them to stop focusing on those things exclusively and to focus for awhile on what is at the heart of life, on God. In our society, it seems that this is the one thing we are afraid to do with couples, whether their marriages are fine or whether they are in trouble. We'll talk about trust and listening and forgiveness, all of which is fine. But we seldom talk to them about God. Seldom do we tell them that they have come together for a reason. Seldom do we tell them that, instead of being a stumbling block to growth and happiness, their spouse's faults are a precise call to the areas in which *they* (not their spouse) need to grow. Seldom do we tell them that their spouse is part of their mission on earth, that missions are often difficult, and that we are tempted to abandon them just when the going gets tough. Even less often do we walk them through the Bible, showing them that God is the one who has remained faithful to his people, even when time and time again they have wandered far away from him.

Yet this is just the time when people need to know God, need to know him intimately, so intimately that they realize that, as human beings, they are made in his image and likeness. Just when they see the tapestry of their married lives as something horrible and life denying, they need to see that by focusing on the faithfulness of God, they can, with his help, reweave that tapestry into something beautiful.

I have seen new life spark in marriages when I have had people reflect on the fourteenth chapter of the Gospel of John, where Jesus says, "I am going to prepare a place for you." (John 14:2). When I ask them, "Do you want to find your special place?" They often nod. "Then look into your spouse's eyes," I tell them.

Finding God, we find everything—the reason for everything, the way to evaluate everything, and the way to deal with everything. The wisdom of God is our attic wisdom.

## 4. In the attic of our soul we have the ability to "dwell a hermit" in any situation.

There's a common myth that says most of us are too busy to pray or to meditate, too busy to take

time to turn to the soul. James Russell Lowell
counters that by saying that we can turn inward
at any time and in any place. This is not to say
that we do not need special times—Sabbath days,
holy days, and special times of prayer. Indeed, we
do. But these days are not just for themselves.
They are meant to help us develop the habit of
turning within frequently throughout the day
and the week. We may have friendships where
we meet one day a week and do not talk to each
other at any other time. But our relationship with
God is not like that. The Bible insists over and
over again that this relationship with God is a
covenant.

Covenants are hard for us to understand,
because we are accustomed to thinking of con-
tracts. In a contract we agree to exchange one
thing for another (usually services for money) for
a definite period of time. After three years, say,
the contract is finished.

Covenants are different. A covenant is a com-
mitment of person to person, heart to heart, not
for a period of time, but forever. Covenants
are twenty-four-hour-a-day, seven-day-a-week

pledges of love. Covenants are still binding even when one person does not hold up his or her end of the bargain. The Bible tells us over and over again that the relationship between God and us is a covenant, not a contract. There are to be no cancellation clauses and no days off. It tells us that when we are not faithful, God is still faithful. It challenges us to be faithful even when we feel that God has abandoned us.

This covenant exists because of who God is and who we are. The message of the fifth soul stage is that we are made for union with God, and that to the extent to which we do not contemplate him and enter into a covenant with him, we are incomplete. Put positively, insofar as we do look for him and for lasting, eternal values and ideals, we are doing what we were meant to do, living as we were meant to live.

The notion of a covenant is important for this fifth stage of the soul. We have spoken of crossing a threshold into the stage of attic wisdom. The Hindu notion of *satori* will be familiar to some, and it has the same meaning—to cross a threshold. You can't be both inside the house and outside the house at the same time; to enter the house, you must cross a threshold. Once we have broken past the fleeting values and goals that we have been considering our be-all and end-all, once we have begun to look at eternal values and the God who is behind them, we are no longer the same. We may—and do—forget our soulful glimpse at the ideals and turn again to the lure of the everyday. Like the prodigal son, we leave home, in the illusion that our inheritance lies somewhere else; then we long to find our way back again. And like the prodigal son, we know where home is, because we have been there once. That is what a covenant does: it changes you forever. Once you have basked in the sunlight of the eternal, you may leave, but you are never the same. The light of the eternal always shines within you, calling you back into itself. In a covenant, you are never again left alone.

Like the prodigal son, we can begin our journey back home wherever we are. We do not need to be in a monastery or even in a quiet place. We can return home in the midst of the dishes, with the hungry kids or the difficult boss, or on the evening commute. As we have noted before, your soul is where you are. You can find it anywhere.

### 5. You can do it. Attic wisdom is as much for you as it is for a monk in a monastery.

The soul stage of attic wisdom is not something that is just for "trained religious" or "specialists" or "experienced" people. Each and every one of us is called to bask in the light of eternal truths and values. "The eyes are the window to the soul" is an expression that tells us that soulfulness and attic wisdom are meant for everyone.

It's not complicated, either. As you learn to ask yourself, "What do I really want in this situation?" and as you grow to realize that what you really want is not just tangible and material, but also eternal and spiritual, you are getting somewhere.

You can do it. Attic wisdom is not above you or beyond you. It does not take more time than you have, and it does not require a complicated set of equipment. Your willingness is the key that unlocks the attic door.

# *Return—Coming Back to the World You Left*

Once you have gone into the attic, it is tempting never to come out again. You can build a cozy little nest there, sitting and contemplating and playing. I remember the times I made the thirty-day spiritual exercises of St. Ignatius Loyola. Whether made on the then-spacious grounds of St. Stanislaus Seminary in Florissant, Missouri, or in the autumn lushness of a retreat house in

Cornwall, New York, these times were nothing short of spectacular. They weren't perfection— some days were long and all of us retreatants were facing serious life issues—but they were times for a freeze-frame. Eastern Missouri and the Hudson Valley produce equally beautiful autumns, with cool breezes and leaves riotous with color. We had the whole day to meditate in silence, to walk about, to be free from business and conversation. We spent thirty straight days contemplating the eternal.

Wisely, our retreat directors scheduled some bridge days before sending us back into the world after those experiences. I can't speak for all of us, but for myself, I could have stayed in retreat forever. To have plunged directly into the harsh realities of everyday life would have been a cruel immersion. Those interim days led us gently into the inevitable truth that we must, after all, come back to the world we had left a month before. We could not stay in our spiritual attics.

Modern psychology tells us that we men are particular builders of attics or caves in which to hole up and figure out our lives. I'm not sure that is true. Women, too, need their nests, their nooks, their quiet corners in which to break from their harried days. We all need our places of respite, but we also need to return.

It's difficult to return, and that difficulty is classic. "It is easy to go down to Avernus," the Sibyl of Cumae warned Aeneas as he prepared to visit the underworld. "But to retrace your steps and come back to upper air, this is difficult, this is labor." Ulysses found he had a long journey home once the wars were over. Thomas Wolfe made the return home an utter impossibility: "You can't go home again." Yet as much as we want to stay in the realm of the eternal, the drive is in us to return to our world. Sooner or later, we must descend the stairs, leave the attic, and return to the living room.

Once you have found your soul and have seen the possibility that its attic wisdom offers, an indelible memory is established. It is not exactly true to say that there can never be any turning back to the ordinary way of looking at things, but it is true to say that the experience of soulfulness is always there as a reminder. It is an experience that can call us back to soulful awareness when the worries and cares of life overcome us.

Cultivated, it is an experience that can make us want to live soulfully and no other way.

Though our souls draw us upward, they inevitably lead us back into everyday life. Plato's philosopher, safely ensconced among the eternal ideas, was destined to return to the cave to tell his former colleagues there about the world he had discovered. There is both destiny and tragedy in this, however; the prisoners did not want to hear his message and tried to put him to death. Could Plato have been thinking of his beloved mentor Socrates, whose teaching led him to be put to death on charges of corrupting the youth of Athens?

It is true. Our quest for a deeper soulfulness, as we have seen it, has been a quest for peace, and the entry into soulfulness that makes lasting peace possible can change our lives. But then, the soul makes a hard demand. Having experienced the magic of soul, we are now asked to go back into the world from which we came—the world of ordinary life—and to live soulfully there. Somehow, the soulful life is incomplete unless the soul returns to the world that it thought it had left.

In sending us back to the world, the soul teaches us a number of important lessons.

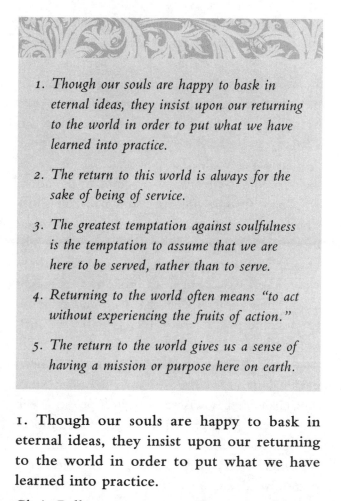

1. *Though our souls are happy to bask in eternal ideas, they insist upon our returning to the world in order to put what we have learned into practice.*

2. *The return to this world is always for the sake of being of service.*

3. *The greatest temptation against soulfulness is the temptation to assume that we are here to be served, rather than to serve.*

4. *Returning to the world often means "to act without experiencing the fruits of action."*

5. *The return to the world gives us a sense of having a mission or purpose here on earth.*

**1. Though our souls are happy to bask in eternal ideas, they insist upon our returning to the world in order to put what we have learned into practice.**

Chris Bell was a nice young man working at Covenant House in New York City, a renowned

center for troubled and runaway youths. His zeal
and generosity toward the kids were the hallmark
of Chris's presence there. A friend recalls seeing
a pair of boots that Chris had received from his
parents finding their way onto the feet of a
homeless kid who didn't have shoes. That was
Chris.

Chris was troubled at Covenant House. More
and more he saw teenage girls come to the house
who had become pregnant and had had abortions. As he spoke with them, he was dismayed
to see how readily society pressured them into
having abortions, letting them feel that there
was no alternative. His heart broke at the thought
of the helpless lives that had been ended and at
the terrible psychological effects upon the girls
themselves.

Chris's "attic" since his college days had been
personal prayer and the assistance of Father Benedict Groeschel, a wise and soulful priest. Week
after week, Chris prayed about the young mothers and their unborn children. He became increasingly angry that so many lives were being
tragically ruined. Week after week, he would rant
and rave to Father Benedict, "How can society let

this happen? How can we do this to these women and their children?"

One day, a remark from Father Benedict effectively booted Chris out of his attic and changed the course of his life. After hearing the usual round of raving and complaining, Father Benedict cast a piercing look into the eyes of the young man sitting before him and said, "Chris, if you are going to do so much complaining about this problem, why don't you do something about it?"

That simple question was enough to change the focus of Chris's life. He went to work and established Good Counsel Homes, the first in Hoboken, New Jersey, where single pregnant women could stay while they were preparing to have their babies, and where they could engage in a year-long program of parenting, counseling, and the development of work skills so that they could mother and support their babies by the year's end. That was fifteen years ago. Today, there are numerous Good Counsel Homes established in New York, New Jersey, and Connecticut, run by Chris and a dedicated staff. What countless lives have been saved and turned around thanks to the committed work of one young man who accepted the fact that his soul was calling him out of his attic of praying and complaining into a whole new way of touching the world!

## 2. The return to this world is always for the sake of being of service.

The soul has as its purpose and mission the task of bridging the world of the eternal and the everyday world in which we live. Once it leads us out of the limitations of our lives as citizens of this world and allows us to spend some time as citizens of the kingdom within, it marches us back into our former world and tells us to help it to build the bridge.

I was sitting at the console at WABC Radio early one Sunday morning, reading the mail before going on the air on "Religion on the Line." I noticed a flyer for a book called *The Pummeled Heart: Finding Peace through Pain* by Antoinette Bosco. I put it aside and, quite frankly, forgot about it. About a year later, I arrived in the Telicare studios on Long Island to be the guest of Frank De Rosa on his television program, "Point of View." When I walked into the

library, Frank greeted me and introduced me to
Antoinette Bosco, who was also there to tape a
show and to discuss her new book, *Coincidences*.
That "coincidental" meeting led to Toni and I
becoming friends, and to my hearing her remarkable story of heartache turned to mission. The
heartache would take your breath away. It included a difficult marriage and divorce, then the
tragic murder of a son and his wife, and the suicide of another son. As I listened to her story, I
wondered how any one person could withstand
so much unspeakable tragedy.

Toni certainly had her time in the attic, rumi-
nating about life and love and about what had
happened to her. What was remarkable was that
her soul kept calling her to go back out into life
again, to do something positive about each of the
things that had happened to her. She started one
of the first groups in her area for separated and
divorced Catholics in order to bring comfort and
support to people like herself who had gone
through the pain of divorce and separation. Separated and divorced Catholics often feel a special
sense of isolation, anger, and failure; and sadly,
misinformation has led many of them to believe
that they can no longer be active Catholics.

Working from her own experience as a divorced mother, Toni decided to provide a place where people like herself could meet and talk and feel the comfort of God's presence and the support of the Church as they tried to put their shattered lives back together.

What happened next was even more amazing. The loss of her two sons and her daughter-in-law was devastating. Yet, even in this, Antoinette Bosco heard her soul calling her not to give up, but to go out. She decided to tell the story of her losses in the hope of helping others who had sustained excruciating losses themselves. Today, she is a respected and talented journalist and author whose lectures and guest appearances on radio and television have given heart to so many who thought they would never feel encouraged again.

"I still get very angry with God sometimes," Toni told me once. "But I have learned that God is someone I can trust. I can put my hand into his, even when I don't understand or agree with where he is leading. But there's more. As time went on, I discovered that I needed to think about a legacy for my sons and daughter-in-law. I decided that my life would be their legacy. I would, through my writing and in whatever other way I could, try to give understanding and hope to others who experienced pain in their lives. That would be the legacy I would create for my children. If there were to be any sense in what happened to them, I would have to make that sense by using their stories—and mine—to help others."

It was not enough for Antoinette Bosco to make peace with God. Deep within her, she needed to return to the world that had treated her and her dear ones so cruelly, to be of service.

### 3. The greatest temptation against soulfulness is the temptation to assume that we are here to be served, rather than to serve.

Service is the key to the sixth stage of the soul. The soul brings you back into the world from which you came. And when you return, you come to be of service to the world by finding a way to bridge the gap between it and the eternal. The concept of service is essential if the soul is to fulfill its purpose in the world. For there are two ways of emerging from the attic. One is to be of service. The other is to demand that we be the ones who are served.

Once we have scaled the heights of the ideals, it is tempting for us to think that we are special and deserving of some out-of-the-ordinary reverence or honor or respect. The second type of exit from the attic is a tragic one because it sets back the progress of the soul. Here, the ego kicks in and demands that it be the center of attention, that it be the object of the world's attention. I'm sure we have all seen people who have set themselves up as experts, idealists, or holy men and women having some kind of credentials or special knowledge that others do not. It is hard to get through life without meeting people who think they are the "be-all and end-all," and who expect the rest of us to respond accordingly. I have done it myself on occasion, and never has it accomplished anything for me, except to make me look very silly. My father said it best in a homily he delivered to me several decades ago: "My boy, whenever in life I have put myself higher than I should, life has always managed to knock me down to size."

The plain truth is we are not here to be served by others, and we are not here to serve ourselves. Thinking otherwise is a first-class ticket back to square one—being a lost soul. The prophets of the great religions have had a common idea: whoever wants to be the greatest must serve the rest.

The soul cannot stand an ego that insists upon being unto itself. In the *Baghavad Gita*, the god Krishna tells Arjuna that he must go to war, whether he likes the idea or not. It is his duty and he must serve regardless of whether he thinks he is getting anything out of it. In the Gospels, Jesus rebukes Peter, who thinks that it is above Jesus's dignity to suffer.

In the Book of Judges in the Hebrew Bible, there is a wonderful story about the day the trees decided to select one of their number to be their king. It is a magnificent rendering of the difference between ego and soulful service. As the story goes, when the olive tree was approached about becoming king of the trees, it answered, "Should I give up my oil, by which both gods and men are honored, to hold sway over the trees?" The fig tree, when approached, said, "Should I give up my fruit, so good and sweet, to hold sway over the trees?" Then the trees approached the vine, who said, "Should I give up my wine, which cheers both gods and men, to hold sway over the trees?" Only the thorn bush agreed, saying, "Come, and take refuge in my shade." (Judg. 9:9–15)

The temptation to be served rather than to serve is enormous. Any of us can fall prey to it. In supermarkets, filling stations, reception desks, doctor's offices, dare I say even churches, it is all too common to find a lack of the concept of service. We all get tired. We all forget why we are here. But we are not happy when we do.

The soul insists that we are not here to be served, but to serve. We are here to bring to the world something of eternity because we know that otherwise, the world and the souls that fill it would not so easily find their meaning and fulfill the purposes of their journeys.

## 4. Returning to the world often means "to act without experiencing the fruits of action."

Service is a tricky thing. One of the tests of soulful service is our ability to keep on giving it when it seems that we are not getting anything in return. As a priest, I have been called to what were once known as the "back wards" of hospitals to visit babies who were born with severe deformities. There is not much heroism in my occasional visits to these precious little ones. But there is great heroism in the doctors, nurses, and aides who faithfully love these babies whose parents often have abandoned them. Day after day, they bathe them, feed them, and love them, often receiving little or no response. That doesn't seem to matter to them, somehow. The love is palpable there. When I think of the famous moral of the *Gita*: "Act without experiencing the fruits of action," my mind goes to those dedicated souls who give love day in and day out, and who would never dream of living any other way.

Sometimes when the return of love does come, it comes slowly or after a very long time.

I was talking recently to my friends Sister Raymond Dieckman and Sister Rita Redmond, Ursuline Sisters from Paola, Kansas. They taught me Latin and English at Bishop Miege High School in Kansas City, Kansas, and have been role models and dear friends ever since. In the course of our conversation, Sister Rita told me a story that began with a terrible fall she had when she tripped while carrying some dishes in the convent dining room. Badly cut and sustaining multiple broken bones and injuries, she was rushed to the emergency room of a nearby hospital. She emerged, hours later, heavily bandaged and bruised and in great pain. She seated herself in a chair in the waiting room, while another Sister went to get the car.

"As I waited," Sister Rita recalled, "I noticed a middle-aged man with shoulder-length gray hair. He looked at me, and came over to me.

"'You're an Ursuline Sister, aren't you?' he asked me.

"Yes I am," I replied, wondering who he was.

"'I went to Bishop Miege High School,' he said, and told me his name. I remembered him and recalled that he had probably only attended our high school for a year or so.

"He continued, 'When I went to Miege, there were three people who helped me. They made me believe that I was a good person and that I had something to offer to the world. That had never happened to me before. I will always remember Father Sullivan (the principal), Mr. Frazier (science teacher and football coach), and Sister de Lourdes.'"

At this point in the story, it is important to mention that after the changes in the Catholic Church in the 1960s, many Roman Catholic Sisters went back to using their own names rather than the religious names they had taken years before. The man who approached Sister Rita in the emergency room that night did not realize that the heavily bandaged nun he was addressing was actually the Sister de Lourdes of his high school days, the very nun who had made him feel so special.

"I didn't say anything," Sister Rita told me, "but there must have been a gleam in my eyes. He said to me, 'You are Sister de Lourdes.'

" 'Yes, I am,' I replied. He came closer to me, bent down, and kissed me on the cheek. Just then, Sister was ready with the car, and he walked me to the car and helped me in."

I have known Sister Rita and Sister Raymond since my own high school days, some forty years ago. I know how hard they worked as teachers, how much they gave of themselves, and how little they often received from us in return. What a testimonial to the power of love, some thirty years after Sister Rita touched this man's life. He showed up in the emergency room, found her, and was able to express his appreciation to her, just when she needed it most.

## 5. The return to the world gives us a sense of having a mission or purpose here on earth.

While this statement is true, I want to resist the temptation to make it sound too elitist or grandiose. The words "mission" and "purpose" are often the sorts of terms we apply to "Really Noble Causes," such as founding the Red Cross or starting a religious movement. The truth is, when the soul sends us back into the world to bridge the eternal or the temporal, it often has us do very mundane things.

I have often been grateful for the training I received as a Jesuit novice, when I entered the Society of Jesus after college. Though I eventually left the Jesuits to become a priest of the Archdiocese of New York, I learned some important things from the Jesuits, some of which have lasted a lifetime (so far).

One of those lessons was never articulated during our training, but was taught to us between the lines: none of us was either more important or less important than the next guy. Whether you were fresh out of high school or were a college graduate like me, you were treated the same. You were expected to pray when you were supposed to pray, work when you were supposed to work, play when you were supposed to play. You might have been a Rhodes Scholar (I was not), but you were still expected to take your turn at cleaning the bathrooms and visiting the sometimes-cranky older priests in the infirmary. No job was too good for you or beneath you. Like it or not, you were expected to do it all, to do it cheerfully, and to do it to the best of your ability.

Why? Because according to the Jesuit logic, every human being, no matter how young or old, great or small by human standards, has the noble purpose of working for the greater glory of God. If you thought you were too good to peel potatoes or wash dishes, you had a lot to learn about the glory of God.

That is why I get a little uneasy about philosophies and programs that imply that menial tasks are demeaning and should be risen above. There's nothing demeaning about raking a yard or holding down a blue-collar job. Working for many

years in parishes in the borough of Manhattan, I
have met people who, by force of circumstance or
by choice, will always have menial, hard, blood-
sweat-and-tears jobs, and who are able to go to
work each day because they are sustained by a
deep and fervent life of prayer. They pray hard
and work hard and do their utmost to make their
hard work something wonderful for God. These
are people with a mission, and their mission is
just as real and just as important as are those of
heads of states, captains of industry, and leaders of
religions.

Over my two decades of living in New York
City, I have come to have deep respect for New
York City cab drivers. Patrick Coyne is one of
the reasons.

I thought I was getting in touch with Patrick
for the first time when my friend June LeBell of
WQXR told me about him. June mentioned how
she had serendipitously ridden with Patrick on
three occasions and had come to know of his love
for people and his deep faith. Now, she told me,
Patrick, retired and living in Mississippi, had cancer. I asked June if I could send him my book
and she kindly arranged to have an autographed
copy sent to him.

I was delighted when, a few weeks later, I received a handwritten letter from Patrick, thanking me for the book. I was surprised to learn that he had been a regular listener to my radio program, "As You Think," and that he had attended one of my Masses at Our Lady of Peace Church. His letter repeated my homily back to me! Better still, Patrick revealed to me that we had actually met. When he recounted the incident, I remembered: he shook my hand at the back of the church and gave me a twenty-dollar bill as a contribution to my radio ministry. Imagine, a cabbie giving *me* a tip!

Patrick had a deep religious conviction, but it didn't stop at the church door. It permeated his taxicab. Patrick told me that as a New York City cabbie, he felt a need to make everybody who got into his cab feel better. If he noticed that someone seemed down or depressed, he tried to give him or her hope and encouragement. This was not a random phenomenon, nor was it accidental; Patrick made this his personal mission.

That is why I am disinclined to make the concept of mission or life purpose too highfalutin. Putting together what the Jesuits taught me with what Patrick taught me, none of us is more or less important than anybody else, and the most menial of tasks can be done in such a way as to give inspiration.

The Sibyl of Cumae was right: it's hard to come back to earth after having been conversant with the eternal. But come down to earth we must. And if we never quite feel at home there, that's okay. We know where home is—and we know why we're here.

# Re-enchantment—Teaching Our Hearts to Sing Again

The return to everyday life can be accompanied by a variety of feelings and emotions, ranging from exhilaration to deep disappointment. On the one hand, there can be the thrill of returning to old places and to loved ones—the joy of returning to where we came from. We see everything with eyes transformed by a new vision. When I came back from each of my thirty-day retreats, I realized that I was seeing the world in a different way. Thirty days of deep contemplation, ending with the sense that everything in my life was the outpouring of God's love, gave my world a sense of excitement.

Not long after leaving the retreat period of my novitiate, I was sent to work as an orderly in a senior residence run by the Little Sisters of the Poor in Kansas City. The hours were long and the manual work was something that I was not entirely suited for. Despite that, the retreat had endowed me with the sense that God had brought me there for a reason. That realization enabled me to endure the difficulties while being buoyed by the endearing presence of the elderly residents and the simple beauty of the Sisters. As I say, the residents were endearing, though not always easy to cope with. In the men's dining room, where I was assigned, there was an irascible old fellow named Jerry, who often ambled about like a windup doll, bellowing, "Vy me?" in a thick German accent. If we were able to take Jerry with humor, it was largely because of dear Adolph, a gentle giant of a man whose warm laughter and occasionally ribald stories made him the de facto head of the dining room. Keeping us all on the program was Joe Riley, an affable old man who had been in the home for years. Joe knew the home and its systems like a book, and he made sure that the rest of us knew that we were supposed to follow the rules. With those wonderful gentlemen around me, it was easy to keep a sense of adventure and even excitement alive in the midst of the daily routine.

My re-entry to the world after thirty days of retreat was rather blissful. Not everyone has such a happy return. A woman told me once about an unhappy life she had prior to enduring an almost fatal illness. At a critical point in her hospitalization, she told me, she experienced what she called a "near-death" experience. She said she felt her soul rising above her body. Shortly thereafter, she said, she underwent a guided review of her life; and she eventually came to bask in a beautiful light. This, she told me, was the most blissful experience of her life. With all her heart, she wanted to remain in this warm and radiant presence. To her disappointment, she was told that there was still work for her to do on earth, helping her loved ones and others to know that there was life after death, and they need not be afraid.

"I know I have an important mission," the
woman told me, explaining that her life was full
as a writer, counselor, speaker, and family member. "But every day, I regret with all my heart that
I am not back with that blissful presence. I wish
I were back there. I feel so utterly incomplete."

Re-entry into everyday life can be, well,
just re-entry. In fact, for all of us there comes a
point where our daily round becomes just everyday. Who of us has not taken that special vacation, only to find life waiting for us when we
returned? Personally, one of my least favorite
tasks upon returning from vacation is going
through the mail. No matter how buoyed or
rested I have been on vacation, sorting through
the mail can truly put me out of sorts. The junk
mail is relatively easy to deal with, but then there
are the bills and the troublesome letters that
demand attention. After the mail, there are the
telephone messages that have piled up, and the
E-mails. Before I know it, life is upon me, and I
am left wondering where vacation went. Was it
only this time last week that I was so peaceful and
rested?

All my life, it seems, I have wrestled with the problem of re-entry. At times, I have lived in places in which I was utterly depressed. I would go away for a week or a weekend, wondering, "How can I bring the joy of this vacation with me when I go back?" Upon arriving home, I would realize that once again I was back in the same place, not just physically, but emotionally as well.

It was years before I realized that I was not the only one who had this problem. It took me much longer to discover the possibility of reenchantment.

Thomas Moore taught me the word in our many chats on "As You Think" and in his magnificent book *The Re-Enchantment of Everyday Life*. As with every aspect of soulful living, however, learning the word was not enough. I had to discover what it meant to *my* soul, to let it roll over my tongue, to evoke it with my own voice.

The word "re-enchantment" comes from the French word *chanter*. It literally means "to sing again." Once I realized that bit of etymology, it occurred to me that it is the perfect word to describe the problem of how to experience the enchantment found in the stage of attic wisdom once you have found yourself back on earth. The word tells us that to think we can hold on to the bliss found in the attic of our souls is folly. One way or the other, life manages to snuff it out.

What we must look for instead is *re-*enchantment. The prefix *re-* means "again." If we cannot carry the bliss of the attic into the world with us and keep it, can we remember what we experienced then, and, allowing ourselves to lose it, teach our soul to sing its tune?

In the odd twists and turns the soul takes, it was a group of Arapahos who taught me about re-enchantment. Shortly after I was ordained to the priesthood, I spent several weeks at the Wind River Reservation for Native Americans of the Arapaho and Shoshone tribes. Father Carl Starkloff and the other Jesuits at St. Stephen's Mission were concerned that, for many years, indigenous people had been forbidden to practice their religious customs and even to speak their native languages. As a scholar of Native American religions, Father Starkloff realized how crippling these restrictions had been to the tribes and how gravely it had jeopardized their future existence.

He decided to work with the "Old Men," the tribal elders among the Arapahos on the mission, to see whether they could reconstruct their native language. To make the beginning of this process simple, Father Starkloff asked the Old Men to try to compose the Our Father and one of the Eucharistic Prayers of the Catholic Mass in their native language.

I attended a number of the meetings during this process; as I watched, it became clear to me that these tribal elders were not just composing prayers. They were coming alive to memories long buried in the depths of their souls. These memories evoked a dignity and a reverence and a way of life so important to them as individuals and as a tribe.

Sometimes it was a struggle to reconstruct words and concepts. I recall one such effort to remember the Arapaho word for "reconciliation." Every elder had a particular story showing some aspect of "forgive us our trespasses as we forgive those who trespass against us." I remember one of them explaining to me that reconciliation meant that if long ago you had stolen my father's horse, then your son had to give me one of his horses. One word involved the telling of a whole story. It was a remarkable process of stories and disputes and finally common agreement among the elders as to the meaning of each idea.

Then, they had to recall the actual word in their own language. In the case of "reconciliation," the elders could not come up with the word, try as they might. Finally, one of them remembered an old woman who lived on the reservation who would know the word. They asked her and found it.

Watching these Old Men come alive to their innermost language and memories and stories was for me a fascinating lesson in re-enchantment. The elders were literally coming alive to a part of themselves long buried. They were learning to sing again the songs and stories of their heritage, to bring them—and their own souls—to live in ways at once ancient and new. I am told that when, finally, the prayers were reconstructed, there was a palpable joy in the mission church on the day the Eucharist Prayer was said and the Lord's Prayer sung in the Arapaho language.

Many years later, when I was thinking about how people fall in love with life again, how marriages become restored, how hearts silenced by life learn to sing again, I realized that those elders had taught me so much. Regrettably, they could not go back to that earlier time when they lived freely and spoke freely in their indigenous ways. But they could recapture that time in their souls by remembering stories. The stories charmed their souls into awakening memories from those former times, bringing them to life.

That's what re-enchantment is. When souls learn to sing again in the midst of the hardships and bothers of everyday life, it is because they have come into contact with primal memories that stir and awaken them. These memories appear in the face of grim personal moments. When they come, they re-enchant the soul, recall it to its attic wisdom—its focus on eternity—and remind it to stay in love, to refuse to allow the everyday to extinguish what we truly live for.

*✑*

When, after a time of inspiration, we return to everyday life, the bloom soon falls from the rose and we may find ourselves disenchanted. Facing those grim days, we are little inclined to respond favorably to self-talk or to others' exhortations that we "snap out of it," or that we "have so much to be thankful for," or that "others are worse off" than we. We have known bliss and we have lost it. Perhaps bliss was only a temporary rest stop, we tell ourselves—or a cruel lie.

When we feel like that, I'm not sure that there are any how-tos for becoming re-enchanted, any more than it would have worked if someone had ordered the Arapahos to sit down and reconstruct their language.

What does work, however, is a combination of two simple things. The first is the belief, however small or tenuous, that we can stay in love in the midst of everyday life. The second is the establishment of what I call "stations of re-enchantment"—places or pockets of time that enable us to reconnect with the eternal and to "stay tuned" to its beauty and joy.

When we hear the word "stations" we ordinarily think of radio or television stations, but the word really comes from a Latin word meaning "to stand." Its primary meaning is "places to stand on." Catholics have a Lenten devotion known as Stations of the Cross in which fourteen (or in the modern version, fifteen) meditations and prayers concerning the passion and death of Christ are said, each in a different place in the church. With stations of re-enchantment, there would not necessarily be a given number of stations, but rather the identification of special memories, things, or places in our lives (for example, around the home or the office) that evoke a spirit of beauty or joy, a sense of freedom or justice, or any of the other eternal ideals. As I say, there are no fixed rules here; one person's station of re-enchantment may not work for another. Perhaps, like the Arapahos, we can tell stories of places where people have found re-enchantment and have fallen in love with life again.

For many people, a house of worship is a place to encounter God and the eternal and to fall in love with life again. The Church of the Holy Innocents in the Garment District of New York City has a huge wooden crucifix known as the Return Crucifix. In the more than 125 years of the church's existence, countless thousands of people have knelt before that crucifix and have discovered God's loving forgiveness and mercy in their lives. The devotion concerning the Crucifix developed when a soldier, going off to fight in World War I, stopped to pray before the Cross and to ask God's pardon and protection. After he returned safely from the war, the soldier devoted his life to God as a monk in a monastery. A thousand people a day, many of them workers in the Garment District, would not think of missing a daily moment in that magnificent church or stopping to pray before that Cross.

Stations of re-enchantment are found everywhere. As I write this, I am in Georgetown, South Carolina, where in a few hours I will witness the marriage of James Riddle and Yvette Cancel-Mounier in St. Mary's, a breathtaking little church in the heart of town. James and Yvette chose that church because it was special to their family. Yvette's stepmother, Sandy Jones, was married in that church and attended there for many years before moving to New York. St. Mary's is a touchstone of faith for their family.

People of other faiths have this experience as well. My friend, the late Seif Ashmawy, once took me to a mosque in the heart of Manhattan where devout Moslems gather at midday to pray to Allah. Houses of worship of all faiths are touchstones of encounter with the eternal. In the midst of busy and difficult lives, people come there to remember their true language—the language of soul.

Radio and television can act as stations of re-enchantment. I am amazed to hear from my various audiences how they turn to programs such as mine for inspiration and uplift. Talk programs (such as mine), religious services broadcast over the airwaves, and programs of religious music are places of encounter with the divine for people whose illnesses and heartaches and distance from the flow of life make them feel isolated from anything sacred or precious or divine. One early Christmas morning, after broadcasting the Midnight Mass from St. Patrick's Cathedral on the radio, I went to the apartment of some friends to celebrate the feast. Chatting with the doorman, I learned that he had tuned in to the broadcast on his little radio right there at the reception desk of his building. "I never miss the Midnight Mass," he told me. "Though I am working, it makes me feel like it's Christmas."

Gardens are another station of re-enchantment—wonderful ones, indeed. They are color-

ful and transforming oases at times when our lives
have become deserts. We all have our favorites.
In the midst of my theology studies, I would visit
a rose garden in Berkeley, California, and later
during graduate studies, the Botanical Gardens in
the Bronx. I would have my soul uplifted by the
radiant floral beauty. As a young couple, my parents nurtured wonderful flower and vegetable
gardens; throughout their marriage, my mother
cherished her colorful African violets. Not a
week went by when my father did not arrive
home with roses for my mother. Flowers are very
special angels that remind us of beauty even in
the worst of times.

Flowers remind me of paintings and photo-
graphs as stations of re-enchantment, because
my father loved to photograph flowers and his
mother before him loved to paint them. My
Grandmother Keenan died when I was two, and
I have little recollection of her. But, throughout
my childhood, I knew the beauty of her soul
through her lovely still lifes. I still have a ceramic
vase of hers—a candy jar—and many of my
father's pictures of gardens and flowers. They are

like little gifts from heaven to which I can turn on dark days to refresh my soul.

I love art and paintings, and among those on my office wall is a painting of an old sea captain, pipe in mouth, which hung on our wall at home for many years. That, an envelope full of snapshots from my childhood, and my parents' engagement and wedding album return me to the joy of yesteryear.

Music is another station of re-enchantment. Whether broadcast or performed live in concert, music transports the soul to the very heights and depths of beauty. Music is a strange enchantress, for she sometimes inspires us by taking us to the very limits of our dark side—and beyond. I cannot hear Celine Dion's recording of "My Heart Will Go On" without thinking of my dear friend Susan Bitwinski and her painful death of cancer at age thirty-five. That theme from *Titanic* was one of Susan's favorite songs. For awhile, after her death, I refused to listen if that song came on the radio. Once I decided to go ahead and listen, I realized that though the music brought me to the raw edge of sorrow, it eventually took me to an inner peace and to the knowledge that my love for Susan could still give life—and that Susan was forever okay. Music heals us and reassures us by taking us beyond the edge of sadness.

Music can indeed be a gift from heaven, a message from eternity. While I did not know the classical pianist Samuel Sanders personally, I knew people who did, and our mutual friends had for months been asking me to pray for him as once again he battled serious cardiac illness. When he died, I felt that I had lost a friend. This morning, during my visit to South Carolina, I tuned in a public radio station. How touched I was to hear a tribute to Sam featuring him speaking and performing! It was as though Sam were thanking me for the prayers and letting me know that he was all right.

Books and magazines, prose and poetry of all sorts can lift us heavenward and re-enchant us. When she was a young woman, my mother pasted into her books bookplates whose inscription read "There is no frigate like a book," quoting Emily Dickinson. Seeing my mother's books as a young boy, I learned at an early age not only to read, but also to be transported by books to the pearly gates of feelings and ideas—and beyond. In California and Missouri, Boston and Connecticut, Florida, New Orleans, and South Carolina, I have spent hours admiring waterways and marveling at the varieties of boats and ships that traverse the horizon. Literature, too, has multifarious frigates (novels, romances, epics, histories, tragedies, comedies, scriptures, sonnets, and so on), each bearing its unique cargo and spiriting us off like stowaways to an adventure in the eternal.

The sea can be a tremendous source of re-enchantment. During the awful hours of waiting for word about the fate of John F. Kennedy, Jr., his wife, Carolyn, and his sister-in-law, Lauren Bessette, Ethel Kennedy and several other members of the Kennedy family went sailing. The eternal touch of sea and wind breathed a breath of fresh air into their sad souls, giving them the courage to go on waiting and to deal with the tragedy that lay ahead.

There are many other stations of re-enchantment. I could speak of animals and food, both of which I love very much. My cats, Teddy and Flicka (ages seventeen and twenty-five at this writing), would never forgive me for not mentioning them. And indeed they open wide to me the humor, ingenuity, and love of God. Perhaps, though, we can allow these instances to serve as springboards for you to name your own stations. As the Bible says, the harvest is plenty.

✍❧

Two things are essential for re-enchantment to occur.

First, you must identify stations of re-enchantment in your life. Reading mine can suggest what yours might be, but you must name your own. It is good to name several, to keep a number of channels open to the eternal. At various times, some will touch you more than others. Naming them—writing them down to see—will enable you to be surprised at how many you have at your disposal already. Recognizing our stations of re-enchantment is not so much about taking up new hobbies and interests as it is about taking full advantage of the ones that are already there. King Midas was fatefully focused on creating gold he didn't have. How much more satisfied he would have been had he realized the genuine treasure that was already at his disposal.

Second, you must regularly—daily if at all possible—put yourself in the presence of the stations of re-enchantment which you have identified. Our soulful frigates are not meant to be exceptions to our way of life, but an integral part of it. Why do we insist on praying only on the Sabbath (if then) instead of every day? Why do we fuss over people's birthdays and forget to honor them and love them throughout the year? The gift of re-enchantment is something that we must cultivate daily if we are to be soulfully re-enchanted ourselves.

Re-enchantment means taking time. Steven Covey has remarkably documented how we fill our lives with things to be done, then "relax" with things that don't really engage us. To live lives of re-enchantment, we must purposely put ourselves in the presence of things that re-enchant us. You don't have to be a pagan to know that if you ignore the gods—the daily harbingers of the soul—you will stop noticing them.

That doesn't mean that the gods (using that term loosely) will stop appearing or stop beckoning to you. They will beckon, and somewhere in your soul you will hear their call as a frustration. Allow enough frustration to build and, before long, you will be a lost soul again.

There is no need for that. Name your stations of re-enchantment and allow them—at least some of them—in every day. Before you know it, you will be re-enchanted with life.

# Perambulations

## *Meandering Through the Soulful Life*

I hope that you have found this walking tour of the soul both profitable and pleasant. For that is what you and I have undertaken together. On a journey, we mark points along the way, spots where our journey took a turn, or something special happened, or we encountered some bit of significant flora or fauna or landscape along the way. That is what you and I have done on this journey of the soul. We set out actually as lost souls, not knowing where we were or where we were going, and made our way to a point where we were re-enchanted with life.

In the beginning, we thought that we were all alone on our journey, undertaking something that no one had ever done before and could not possibly understand. Gradually, it surprised us to see that others had left their footprints before ours, near ours. By getting a glimpse of their stories, it dawned on us that what we were experiencing was not as strange and outlandish as we had first believed. We discovered that there was comfort in being lost, so long as we were not the only ones lost, so long as we had company.

This was a new realization for us. Previously, we had been led to imagine that soulfulness, like so many of the other icons of success today, might come to us at the end of a process. Get out of your present misery by following this or that series of steps and you can become soulful. Then we learned to believe otherwise. "Your soul is where you are," we said. This means that there is no aspect of our lives, from the moment of our conception on, that is not soulful.

We might ask whether this makes any difference. If I am a lost soul or am falling through the cracks, is that experience necessarily better, just because it is soulful?

There are several ways of responding to this. One is that soulfulness is not about making our unpleasant and painful experiences less painful or less unpleasant. Re-enchantment, in fact, can coincide with great pain. A loss can spawn a sense of wonder and bemusement, yet still be painful. Soulfulness is not about fixing or correcting or repairing anything. In a recent homily, I alluded to the fact that in my life, there have been mornings when I simply have not felt like getting out of bed to face the day. After Mass, an older gentleman approached me. "Father," he said, "what you said about not wanting to face the day—that's me. The older I get, the harder it is for me to get up in the morning." Now, his experience and mine are just as soulful as those of people who leap joyously out of bed every morning. Theirs are not more soulful and ours are not less soulful or unsoulful. Theirs are not better than ours, nor are ours worse than theirs. Both are real, both are soulful.

In different persons and situations, the soul
can work its magic in very different ways. Sometimes, it inspires us to manifest the gift of fortitude—the courage to get out of bed, slay the
dragons, and fulfill our purpose today. At other
times, it may ask us to have the courage to stay in
bed and address head-on the questions it may be
posing to us in our resistance to facing the day. In
other words, the difference that soulfulness makes
lies in the recognition that the moments of our
lives are not unto themselves alone, but are meant
to embrace the eternal ideals, such as courage,
truth, justice, and love, and to evoke those ideals
in our responses to them. Without the soul, our
lives would be series of unconnected dots. It is
the soul that unifies those moments not by making them the eternal, but by evoking the eternal
in the face of them.

What if we fail in life? Is failure soulful?
Again, the fundamental answer is that the soul is
always there, even when we fail.

The answer depends in part, though, on what
we mean by failure. At one point in my academic
career, I failed one of my graduate comprehen-

sives. That was clearly a failure, and I felt like a failure. Eventually, I sensed that my soul was using that failure as a signal to me to get out of the doctoral program and to move into parish work (which I saw pretty quickly) and eventually into life as a diocesan priest, radio talk show host, and writer (down the road). That failure, then, turned out to be a message. True failure would have meant neglecting my soul's urgings in the direction of my true mission. In another person, however, failing the comps might be the soul's challenge to redouble his or her efforts, work harder, and persist in getting the degree and pursuing an academic career. In the latter case, not following the soul's lead would be failure.

What about moral failure? The ramifications of moral failure for soulfulness are the subject of another book. But, in general, we can say that the task of the soul is to bring our temporal condition to the bar of the eternal. That is the function and purpose of the soul. Moral failure means deliberately choosing to ignore or to misapply eternal principles to our concrete situation. When that happens, the soul moves in to promote remorse and better moral understanding. It is possible for us to ignore the soul's guidance, even to the point of eventually convincing ourselves that what we are doing is right. Even when it is ignored, the soul continues to exert its positive moral influence. The soul refuses to be codependent and continues to send its moral message. How else do we explain the countless stories of people who have "hit bottom," yet in so doing have found their way to a good moral life? I know recovering alcoholics who slip from time to time. When they do, they feel helpless. Yet despite their helplessness they sense a higher power within them gently and firmly calling them back to sobriety.

In all things, the soul works strongly and sweetly, calling us to realize the sacredness that lies within us and our call to express that sacredness in our everyday decisions.

In the final analysis, our trek through the stages of the soul has taught us that no matter how far we may be from God and our divine purpose, none of us is really very far away after all. Our soul is on a course toward enchantment and even re-enchantment. We may try to ignore the soul, but it is still where we are—it never goes away. Our choices may send us back to prior stages of being lost, but the soul is there just the same, cajoling us, exhorting us, reminding us that we are destined for higher things.

Our walking tour of the soul has taught us something about our painful days and our times of depression. Its lessons are very different from the ones we ordinarily hear from the common wisdom. Our painful days, our days of depression, are soulful days. They are not wasted days unless we choose to waste them. They are not days that might become soulful if only we would or could do something to make them so. They are soulful even as we experience them. In our mourning, in our hurt over things someone has done to us, in our times of depression and even despair, the soul is present, watching, noticing, guiding.

In fact, the soul is present in two important ways:

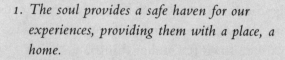

1. *The soul provides a safe haven for our experiences, providing them with a place, a home.*

2. *Once it has gathered our experiences safely into itself, the soul places them before the bar of the eternal, transcendent values, giving us correction, guidance, and sometimes approval.*

Both aspects of the soul's presence are important. Many times in life, we feel that our circumstances are so much bigger than what we can handle. We feel overwhelmed; we feel lost and alone, with nowhere to turn and no one to turn to. What we often fail to realize is that, though we feel scattered and homeless, we are really being called home—not to heaven, but inwardly to the soul. I love what Robert Frost once said in an interview. "I'm not confused," he declared, "I'm just well mixed." Frost knew that his soul was there, taking in his experiences and shifting them around in the wonderfully creative way that contact with the eternal ideas can mix things.

That's why, I imagine, the Latin root of the word "confused" is a word meaning "to mix together." When people discover that fact of language, they are usually startled. How can we be mixed together when it feels like we're falling apart?

The soul is the answer. When life overwhelms us, the soul takes in all of our frustrations, worries, negative responses, hurts, and so on and finds a home for them. They may feel—and we may feel—awkward and displaced, but the truth is, they are not and we are not.

The Bible talks about a farmer who sowed seeds in his field. When he came back to see how the crop was progressing, he discovered that by night someone had sewn weeds in with the wheat, and now wheat and weeds were tangled together all through the field. The man's servants wanted to tear up the weeds, but he wisely refused to let them. "If you tear up the weeds now," he advised them, "you will destroy the wheat as well. Let them grow to maturity, and then we can separate them, saving the wheat and destroying the weeds."

That parable is a story of the soul. The soul takes everything in—our good experiences, our bad experiences, our virtues, our vices, our sins, our successes, everything. It finds a home and a place for them all, then wisely and often slowly, mixes them, bringing depth and wisdom and healing and insight, and urging us to move past what is no longer helpful to us.

That process can take awhile, a fact that can be enormously frustrating to us technological speed demons. Like the farmer's servants, we want to fix things right away. The soul's time is different from our time, and its ways are not our ways. When we see a past strewn with failure and are feeling hopeless, the soul can mix things so that our painful past becomes a source of compassion and insight and a way of serving others. I have seen people shattered by divorce go on to help others who find themselves rocked by the breakup of their marriages. Alcoholics and drug addicts go on to be counselors for those in similar circumstances. It happens more often than we realize.

Perambulations215

It takes time, and that is why it is so important that we know the ways of the soul.

When I flunked my comps and felt so stupid, the bad year I was having reached an all-time low. I wish I had known then what I know now about the soul. It would have been comforting to know that all my feelings of being lost could find a home in my soul, which could sort them out and allow me to learn, to heal, and to discover a new direction.

That's why I'm glad we have taken this tour together. It really helps to know that, appearances to the contrary, all is not lost. Indeed, with your soul at the helm, all is found. Watch, listen, and you'll discover inner compassion and wisdom beyond anything you can imagine right now. Notice, and you'll see people and situations that have been troublesome healing and resolving themselves or passing out of your life. Bless them, and let them go. Pay attention, and you'll see people and circumstances coming into your life that confirm your resolve to be of service, to bring eternal values to your world, and to fall in love with life again.

People have asked me, "Are these steps always progressive and in the order in which you give them?" My experience and reflection on the workings of the soul leads me to believe that the stages do go in the order in which I have outlined them. In my experience, that is the order in which they occur. As I have indicated throughout, it is possible, for a variety of reasons, to fall back to stages 1 and 2, being a lost soul or falling through the cracks. It is also possible to be returned to the world (as in stage 6) or to be re-enchanted (as in stage 7) and to go back for awhile to compassion (stage 3) or to attic wisdom (stage 5). Doing so, in fact, can recharge your batteries and confirm you in your soulful purpose.

Can you move ahead of the order, taking, say, compassion or re-enchantment before being lost? To be honest, I don't think it works that way. Of course, you can educate a child in the eternal virtues, values, and truths at an early age; indeed, such education can be soulful. But that is not quite the same as developing compassion or attic wisdom after having had some experience of heartache in life. What you can do, I believe, is look ahead. At any stage, the soul can give us a glimpse of future stages. Often, this bolsters our faith and hope and helps us to keep going.

☙

When I speak of the soul "mixing" our past and present experiences, people sometimes wonder what this has to do with sins or bad moral choices. They wonder whether I'm saying that, since everything gets sifted out, there is actually no such thing as sin, that the soul just kind of "takes care of it all."

The answer is, I'm not saying that at all. The work of the soul—bridging the eternal and the temporal—depends greatly upon the existence of objective moral ideals and the virtues that empower the soul to act in accordance with them. When we sin, we lay the foundation for bad moral habits, which affect the soul's ability to fulfill its mission. If the soul is trying to reconcile our temporal lives with eternal values and we are deliberately choosing to eschew those values, we make it difficult for the soul to do its work. St. Augustine once used the metaphor of "encrusting" the soul. When we do that, the soul continues to do its work, but we are increasingly less apt to listen to its urgings.

That is why I do not accept those theories of the soul that claim there are genuinely evil souls that are destined to fulfill malignant purposes in the world. Instead, I believe that habit, choice, metabolism, and education can attenuate the soul's fulfillment of its purpose. But I also believe that the soul continues to be in the presence of eternal values, such as goodness, truth, and love, and that it never ceases to let their voices cry out to us. We can choose to fulfill purposes that do not coincide with making the world a better place. But, fundamentally, a soul ignored is not a happy soul.

❧

As I say, I hope you have enjoyed these soulful musings. I believe that we have taken a road that truly matters and introduced a way of life that answers the shallowness of much that passes for success and spirituality and meaning today.

I hope and pray that you will continue to move forward on the journey of your soul, full of grace and replete with re-enchantment.

# Suggested Reading

❧

## Something More

*An Aquinas Reader*, edited by Mary T. Clark. Fordham University Press, 1988.

*A Blue Fire*, by James Hillman. Harper Perennial Library, 1991.

*The Celestine Prophecy*, by James Redfield. Warner Books, 1997.

*Complete Works of Aristotle: Revised Oxford Translation*, by Jonathan Barnes. Princeton University Press, 1984.

*The Confessions of Saint Augustine*, edited and translated by Edward B. Pusey. Modern Library, 1999.

*Fly Fishing: A Life in Mid-Stream*, by Turhan Tirana. Kensington Publishing Corporation, 1996.

*Good News for Bad Days*, by Father Paul Keenan. Warner Books, 1998.

*The Soul's Code*, by James Hillman. Warner Books, 1997.

## Stage One

*The Cambridge Companion to Kierkegaard*, edited by Alastair Hannay and Gordon Daniel Marino. Cambridge University Press, 1997.

*Care of the Soul*, by Thomas Moore. Harper Perennial Library, 1994.

*Companion Through the Darkness*, by Stephanie Ericsson. Harper Perennial Library, 1993.

*Death of a Salesman*, by Arthur Miller. Dramatist's Play Service, 1998.

*My Children, Listen*, by Catherine Helene Toye, M.D. Caritas Communications, Inc., 1998.

*Praying Our Goodbyes*, by Joyce Rupp. Ivy Books, 1992.

*The World's Religions*, by Huston Smith. Harper San Francisco, 1992.

*Your Sacred Self*, by Wayne W. Dyer. Harper Mass Market Paperbacks, 1996.

ᴥ

## Stage Two

*Conversations With God (Book 1)*, by Neale Donald Walsch. Putnam Publishing Group, 1996.

*Earl Nightingale's Greatest Discovery*, by Earl Nightingale and Wayne W. Dyer. Dodd Mead, 1987.

*First Things First*, by Stephen R. Covey. Simon and Schuster, 1994.

*Forgiveness*, by Gerald G. Jampolsky, M.D. Beyond Words Publishing Co., 1999.

*Lights in the Darkness*, by Ave Clark. Resurrection Press, 1993.

*Love Is Letting Go of Fear*, by Gerald G. Jampolsky, M.D. Celestial Arts, 1988.

*Real Magic*, by Dr. Wayne W. Dyer. Harper Mass Market Paperbacks, 1993.

## Stage Three

*The Couple's Companion*, by Harville Hendrix.
Pocket Books, 1994.

*Healing Words*, by Larry Dossey, Harper San Francisco, 1995.

*How to Want What You Have*, by Timothy Ray
Miller. Avon Books, 1996.

*It's Only Too Late If You Don't Start Now*, by Barbara Sher. Delacorte Press, 1999.

*Love, Medicine and Miracles*, by Bernie S. Siegel.
Harper Perennial Library, 1990.

*Men Are from Mars, Women Are from Venus*, by
John Gray. HarperCollins, 1992.

*The Passionate State of Mind*, by Eric Hoffer. Buc-
caneer Books, 1998.

## Stage Four

*The Autobiography of Saint Therese of Lisieux,* translated by John Beevers. Image Books, 1987.

*The Celestine Prophecy*, by James Redfield. Warner
Books, 1994.

*Dogs Never Lie About Love*, by Jeffrey Moussaieff Mason. Random House, 1998.

*Personal Writings*, by Ignatius of Loyola, translated by Joseph A. Munitiz and Phillip Endean. Penguin USA, 1997.

*A Search for God in Time and Memory*, by John S. Dunne. University of Notre Dame Press, 1977.

*The Secret of Shambhala*, by James Redfield. Warner Books, 1999.

## Stage Five

*Complete Works*, by Plato, edited by John M. Cooper and D. S. Hutchinson. Hackett Publishing Company, 1997.

*Creating a Life of Joy*, by Salle Merrill Redfield. Warner Books, 1999.

*Letters and Papers from Prison*, by Dietrich Bonhoeffer. MacMillian Publishing Company, 1997.

*The Lion, the Witch and the Wardrobe*, by C. S. Lewis. HarperCollins Juvenile Books, 1994.

*The Tightrope Walker*, by Dorothy Gillman. Faw-
    cett Books, 1997.
*The Way of All the Earth*, by John S. Dunne. Uni-
    versity of Notre Dame Press, 1978.

## Stage Six

*The Bhagavad Gita*, edited by Juan Mascaro.
    Viking Press, 1983.
*Dumbth*, by Steve Allen. Prometheus Books, 1998.
*Enchanted Love*, by Marianne Williamson. Simon
    & Schuster, 1999.
*Ignatius of Loyola*, by Ignatius, edited by George
    E. Ganss, Paramanda Divakar, and Edward J.
    Malastesta. Paulist Press, 1991.
*Live the Life You Love*, by Barbara Sher. Bantam
    Doubleday Dell Publishing, 1997.
*The Pummeled Heart*, by Antoinette Bosco.
    Twenty Third Publications, 1994.
*The Seven Spiritual Laws of Success*, by Deepak
    Chopra. Amber-Allen Publications, 1995.

## Stage Seven

*A Child's Garden of Verses*, by Robert Louis Stevenson. Harry N. Abrams, 1994.

*Collected Poems of Emily Dickinson*, by Emily Dickinson, edited by Mabel Loomis Todd. Outlet, 1986.

*Dark Night of the Soul*, by St. John of the Cross, edited by E. Allison Peers. Image Books, 1959.

*The Education of the Heart*, edited by Thomas Moore. Harper Perennial Library, 1997.

*The Re-Enchantment of Everyday Life*, by Thomas Moore. HarperCollins, 1997.

## Perambulations

*Coincidences*, by Antoinette Bosco. Twenty Third Publications, 1998.

*The Force of Character*, by James Hillman. Random House, 1999.

*Journey to the Heart*, by Melody Beattie. Harper San Francisco, 1996.

*Leisure*, by Josef Pieper, translated by Alexander
    Dru. Liberty Fund, Inc., 1999.
*Saint Thomas and Epistemology (Aquinas Lecture
    10)*, by Louis-Marie Regis. Marquette Uni-
    versity Press, 1946.
*365 Saints*, by Woodeene Koenig-Bricker. Harper
    San Francisco, 1995.

# Index

Adam and Eve story, 94–96
Aeneas, 165
Aloneness
  falling through the cracks
    stage, 67–68, 76–78
  lost souls, 41–42
Ann's story, attic wisdom
  stage, 133–35
Antitoxin of soul,
  compassion stage,
  93–98
Aquinas, Thomas, 148
Arapahos, 190–91
Archdiocese of New York,
  73, 180
Archimedes, 121
Aristotle, 5, 6
Art, 199
"As You Think" program,
  115
Ashmawy, Seif, 196
Attic wisdom stage, 18–19,
  133–62

Ann's story, 133–35
  covenants and, 158–60
  eternal world, 151–55
  joy and, 149
  Tobit's story, 135–37
  transcendence, 142–45
Attics, 133–41
Augustine, 6
Austen, Jane, 101

Bacchus, 141
*Baghavad Gita*, 175
Barletti, Mary, 126
Bell, Chris, 167–70
Bitwinski, Susan, 199
Bonhoeffer, Dietrich,
  154–155
Book of Judges, 175–76
Bosco, Antoinette,
  170–73
Buddha, 30
Buddhism, 114
Buddhists, 149

Camus, Albert, 34
Cancel-Mounier, Yvette, 196
*Care of the Soul* (Moore), 51
Cathers, Mary Jane, 147
Catholic Church, 29
*The Celestine Prophecy* (Redfield), 116
Chanter, 189
Church of the Holy Innocents, New York, 195
Cirincione, Diane, 102
Clark, Ave, 69–70
Coincidence and tapestry stage, 114–16
Compassion stage, 18, 81–106
 antitoxin of soul and, 93–98
 happiness and, 83
 inner guidance and, 98–103
 inner peace and, 89–92
 intimacy by instinct and, 102
 Mildred's story and, 83–84
 no matter what and, 103–6
 Patrick's story and, 84–88
 peace and, 83–86
 understanding and, 92–93

Covenant House, 167–68
Covenants and attic wisdom stage, 158–61
Covey, Steven, 203
Coyne, Patrick, 182–83

De Rosa, Frank, 170
*Death of a Salesman*, 34, 35, 46
Dickens, Charles, 38
Dickinson, Emily, 200
Dieckman, Raymond, 177–79
Duke University School of Medicine, 22
Dyer, Wayne, 46, 115

Education, 15
Effortlessness and falling through the cracks stage, 73–74
Empathy and tapestry stage, 119–22
End of process, soulful life as, 52–53
Eternal world and attic wisdom stage, 152–56

Failure, 208–9
Falling through the cracks stage, 17–18, 55–79
 aloneness and, 67–68, 76–78
 factors in, 57–68

floating in a vacuum,
61–62
Julie's story and, 59–60
soul place and, 69–70
Tom's story and, 74–76
truth and illusion and,
78–79
world is unfriendly place
and, 64–67
Floating in a vacuum,
61–62
Frankl, Viktor, 155
Frost, Robert, 212

Gardens, 197–98
Gifts of the Holy Spirit, 12
God, names for, 149
"God's Handiwork,"
130–31
Golden Rule, 99
Good Counsel Homes, 169
*Good News for Bad Days*
(Keenan), 16, 84, 93
Groeschel, Benedict,
168–69
Guidance, inner and
compassion stage,
98–103

Happiness, 83
Hoffer, Eric, 93–94, 96
Holmes, Sherlock, 141
Hopkins, Gerard Manley,
148

Immortal soul, 33
Inner guidance and
compassion stage,
98–103
Inner peace and compassion
stage, 89–92
Intimacy by instinct and
compassion stage, 102

Jampolski, Gerald, 102
Jesuits, 180–81
Jones, Sandy, 196
Joy and attic wisdom stage,
149
Joyce, James, 38
Julie's story, 59–60

Keenan, Paul, 16, 84
as lost soul, 26–30
parents, 65–66, 76–77
Kennedy family, 201
KFLO, 130
Kierkegaard, Søren Aabye,
32–33, 35
King Midas, 202–3
Kreyche, Robert J., 105

Lakas, Bob, 36–39, 46
Language of soul and lost
soul stage, 43–47
LeBell, June, 182
*Letters and Papers from
Prison* (Bonhoeffer),
154–155

Life as something to count
on and tapestry stage,
129–31
Literacy, 15
Literature, 201
Little Sisters of the Poor,
Kansas City, 186
Lost soul stage, 17, 21–53
aloneness and, 41–42
language of soul and,
43–47
state of being lost and,
42–43
Lowell, James Russell, 150,
158

Margaret's story, 108–9
Mary, mother of Jesus, 127,
128
McMillan, Dave, 130
Meaning and tapestry stage,
122–29
Melville, Herman, 38
Ménière's disease, 22–23,
24
Midas, King, 202
Mildred's story, 83–84
Mission on earth and return
stage, 180–84
Moby Dick (Melville), 38
Moments of life as teachers
and guides and tapestry
stage, 117–19
Montaigne, 149

Moore, Thomas, 51, 115,
189
Moral failure, 209–10
Mothers Against Drunk
Driving, 147
Music, 199
My Children, Listen (Toye),
22, 23

Native Americans, 190
Nietzsche, 155

Our Lady of Peace Church,
183

Paintings, 199
Passionist Spiritual Center,
Riverdale, New York,
126
Patrick's story, 84–88
Peace, 81
compassion stage and,
83–86, 89–91
Perambulations, 205–18
Plato, 146, 149, 166
A Portrait of the Artist as a
Young Man (Joyce), 38
Presence of soul, 211–17
The Pummeled Heart
(Bosco), 170

Radio, 2, 27, 197
Real Magic (Dyer), 46
Redfield, James, 116

Redfield, Salle, 116
Redmond, Rita, 177–79
*The Re-Enchantment of
Everyday Life* (Moore),
189
Re-enchantment stage, 19,
185–204, 207
Re-enchantment stations,
202–3
"Religion on the Line,"
170
Responsibility, 3
Restlessness, 1–2, 4
Retreats, 163–65, 185–86
Return Crucifix, 195
Return stage, 19, 163–84
to be served and,
173–76
Bell, Chris and, 167–70
mission on earth and,
180–84
service and, 170–73
service without being
served and, 176–80
Riddle, James, 196
Riley, Joe, 187
Rockhurst College, 36, 105
Ron's story, 117–19,
120–21

Saint Francis of Assisi, 91
Sanders, Samuel, 200
Sartre, Jean-Paul, 71
Second Vatican Council, 29

Service and return stage,
170–73
Service without being
served and return
stage, 176–80
Shakespeare, William,
101–2
Sibyl of Cumae, 165, 184
Socrates, 166
Soul
definition of, 5–11
presence of, 211–17
as source of human life,
8–9
stages of, 17–19
Soulful life, 13
as end of process, 52–53
essence of, 1–19
time and, 48–52
St. Augustine, 217
St. Ignatius Loyola, 163
St. John, 126–27
Stages of soul order of, 216
Starkloff, Carl, 190–91
State of being lost and lost
soul stage, 42–43
Stations of the Cross, 194
"Strategies for Living"
program, 130
Sullivan, Bob, 71

Tapestry stage, 18, 107–31
coincidence and, 114–16
empathy and, 119–22

life as something to
count on, 129–31
Margaret's story and,
108–9
meaning and, 122–29
moments of life as
teachers and guides
and, 117–19
Ron's story and, 117–19,
120–21
Terry's story and,
109–13, 119–20
Television, 197
Terry's story, 109–13,
119–20
Time and soulful life,
48–52
*Titanic* (film), 200
To be served and return
stage, 173–76
Tobit's story, 135–37
Tom's story, 74–76
Toye, Catherine Helene,
21–25
Transcendence and attic
wisdom stage, 141–45

Truth and illusion and
falling through the
cracks stage, 78–79
Twain, Mark, 149

Understanding and
compassion stage,
92–93
Universe, truths of,
47–48
University of Arizona at
Tempe, 105

Veronica's story, 25–26

WABC Radio, 170
Wedding feast at Cana,
126–29
Williamson, Marianne, 115
Wind River Reservation,
190
Wonder, state of, 11–13
World is unfriendly place
and falling through
the cracks stage,
64–67